The Positive Thinking Mindset

Unlock Your Potential, Conquer Challenges, Foster Advancement and Success, and Achieve Prosperity to your Fullest Capability

Manjul Tewari

www.manjultewari.com

MASTER YOUR LIFE WITH
THE MASTERY SERIES

Y OU CAN CHECK OUT the other books in the series , "Unleashing to Master the Power Within "below:

Scan   to learn about Ultimate Mindset Mastery Series

Scan this QR code to learn about Ultimate Mindset Mastery Series

Scan this QR Code to learn about Unleashing Mindset Mastery Series

Mindset Mastery Series

To My Parents

Published by Mr. Manjul Tewari
P-24, Engineer Park Apartment, Omega Sector-1
Greater Noida, UP, India 201308

CONTENTS

YOUR FREE GIFT

As a token of my thanks for taking out time to read my book , I would like to offer you a gift.

Download your Free PDF eBook

<u>10 Useful Ways of Talking To Any Body</u>

clicking the link

https://www.manjultewari.com/my-free-e-book/

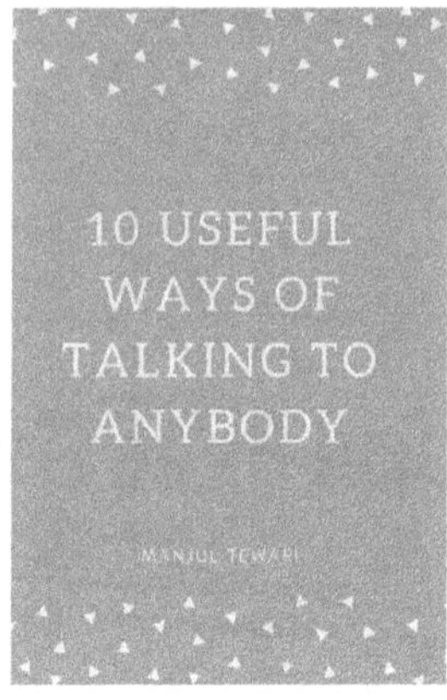

Ten Useful Ways of Talking To Anybody

OR

Scan this QR code to claim your free E Book.

Scan this QR Code

CHAPTER ONE

INTRODUCTION

NICK VUJICIC WAS BORN in Australia in 1982 with no arms or legs, a condition called tetra-amelia syndrome, which is a very rare disorder. Born and raised in Melbourne, Nick suffered from severe physical and emotional obstacles. He was bullied during his childhood; he had a lot of self-doubt and periods of profound despair. Nevertheless, rather than falling victim to the adversity of the situations, Nick developed a power of positive thinking that significantly changed his life.

Having been raised in a world that appeared to be very unsympathetic to his peculiar condition, Nick faced many challenges during his early years. The society's expectations and the glares of the unknown people caused the first feelings of loneliness and self-rejection. Harassment was a burdenful fact, leaving many lifelong scars.

Nevertheless, an important moment symbolized the great change in Nick's thinking. He overcame his greatest fears and made a crucial decision that forever changed his life because of his determination to escape the numerous restrictions his body imposed. It was an extreme change—from concentrating on what he had not, to uncovering boundless opportunities inside.

Nick's growing process also covered his academic endeavors. He pursued a degree in accounting and financial planning at Griffith University with determination. The world of academia, which is usually seen as a place with many hurdles to overcome, became Nick's stage for demonstrating his perseverance in overcoming the many challenges.

The move from the academic world to the world of professional work presented another big challenge. In a society where appearance counts, Nick was constantly denied access to the job market. Nonetheless, his story is not a story of the fall; instead, it is an unmistakable illustration of the flexibility, versatility, and ability to re-define conventional standards.

However, Nick's true calling was born when he developed a deep love for motivational speaking. Understanding the change-making power of sharing his own story, he set out on a quest to give hope to others. This was the beginning of his career as a motivational speaker who reached out to and influenced millions of people all over the world.

The journey of Nick Vujicic took him to more than 60 countries, and he became a symbol of hope for many millions. His charismatic nature, humor-laden and authentic, appealed to people from different walks of life. Nick's message knew no limits, for it was equally preached in the schools and universities, corporate boardrooms and also in religious congregations, his followers forming a global community bound by their common values of hope and determination.

In 2012, Nick married Kanae Miyahara, and they started a new stage in their lives. By transcending the perceptions of society about love and marriage, the union between Nick and Kanae became a true reflection of the universal aspect of the human relationship. Kiyoshi James Vujicic, their first son, was born in 2013, leading the way to a new chapter in Nick's life.

Nick's reach goes beyond mere speaking engagements. He has written many books, including "Life Without Limits" and "Unstoppable," where he gives some very useful tips on how to face problems, keep a positive attitude at all times, and use his own potential. Nick has left a legacy in these literary works, giving the readers a guide to their own quest for personal development.

The way Nick Vujicic has gone through his path is a striking example of the incredible power of a positive thinking mindset—the ability to convert obstacles into opportunity, redefine personal boundaries, and also motivate others to start their own paths of self-development. His story defies stereotypes, promotes resilience, and also calls on people all over the world to accept the endless possibilities of what they could become.

In a world too often ruled by physical looks, Nick Vujicic is a witness to the fact that the real power is rooted in the spirit. His ever-present optimism, resilience, and personal and global transformation are still echoing today, leaving an unremovable stamp on the landscape of human inspiration.

Nick Vujicic's life tells a tale of the unbroken human spirit that ignores the bounds of physical adversity and takes an attitude that converts the obstacles into means of growth and inspiration.

Some major milestones:

Acceptance and Self-Love: Nick embraced himself, understanding his own worth and the fact that it was not only related to the way he looked.

Defying Expectations: Although most people were very skeptical, Nick performed very well at the school, and he even went to college and became a motivational speaker.

Inspiring Others: Nick began to tell his story all over the world and was a source of great inspiration to millions through his speeches as well as his many books.

This man set up the organization Life Without Limbs, which is all about hope and support.

Family and Personal Life: Nick also married and had a son, which illustrates that a positive attitude can lead to very satisfying personal relationships.

Global Impact: Nick's sunny attitude not only changed his life but also touched many people all over the world. His story served as an inspiration for the many challenges.

The life of Nick Vujicic is a treasure trove of deep lessons that resonate with people who are struggling and in search of inspiration

Here are some key lessons drawn from Nick's remarkable journey:

1.The Power of a Positive Mindset:

Nick's life is a living example of what a positive attitude can do. Even though he had to deal with some exceptional physical difficulties, he preferred to concentrate on the opportunities instead of the limitations.

Lesson: Accept positivity in the midst of the challenges. A positive outlook can sculpt your outlook, enrich your adaptability, and create many opportunities from the pitfalls.

Instead of letting the initial challenges of bullying and societal norms define him, Nick decided to be resilient.

Lesson: Resilience is not an opportunity not to have any problems but to recover from them. Embrace failure as a source of your own development.

2.Embracing Self-acceptance:

Nick discovered self-identity within the realms of social norms and expectations. He accepted his difference, knowing that the real power is in being oneself.

Lesson: Accept and rejoice in your own individuality. Self-acceptance is the basis for forming a positive and confident mindset.

3. Turning Challenges into Opportunities:

Nick turned his body's demands into a number of advantages rather than allowing them to defeat him. He continued to gain education, became an inspirational speaker, and then turned into an icon for millions.

Lesson: Often challenges activate a process of development. Go to them with a question and a resilience attitude that looks for the opportunities within the adversities.

4. The Impact of Purpose:

Nick found a sense of mission in inspiring others. The fire of his motivational speaking moved out of himself to create a global influence even greater than his personal battles.

Lesson: Purposeful discovery and preservation define the meaning of life. Recognize your passions and use them to create value for you and others.

5. Building Strong Connections:

Nick's marriage and parenthood are examples of how a person must establish strong bonds. Seemingly, love and family became the focal points of his life, despite social skepticism.

Lesson: Significant relationships make a successful life. Develop relationships by being real, compassionate, and willing to give and help.

6. Transcending Cultural and Geographical Boundaries:

The global influence of Nick as a motivational speaker accentuates the universality of human struggles and the power of inspiration to cross cultural and geographic borders.

Lesson: Our shared human experiences bind us together. The lessons learned from the journey of one person can be felt by people across the world.

7. Perseverance in Pursuit of Goals:

Nick started off receiving job market rejection, but he really bounced back. His persistence to overcome social limitations resulted in the successful career of a presenter.

Lesson: Perseverance is the most important virtue in conquering adversities.

8. Embracing Vulnerability:

Nick's ability to open himself up and share not only his strengths but also his weaknesses brings about an authentic relationship with his audience. He does not wear a mask but, at the same time, considers vulnerability to be power.

Lesson: Accept your weaknesses; they define you as a human. Inspire others to do the same.

9. Overcoming Fear and Stereotypes:

Nick challenged social norms of what a successful life should be. He faced challenges, combated social limitations, and broke the boundaries of what a person with a disability can do.

Lesson: Rebel against societal norms and face your fears.

10. Adapting to Change:

Nick's lifetime was a series of adaptations. From birth to adolescence, marriage, fatherhood, and career, he learned how to accept change with a flexible attitude and adapt to new situations.

Lesson: Life is a dynamic process, and flexibility is essential. Accept changes as a chance for development rather than a threat, and develop the skills of coping with uncertainty.

11. Gratitude in Every Circumstance:

Nick, despite being disabled, thanks the gifts of life. He points out the role of gratitude in focusing on what one has rather than what is missing.

Lesson: Cultivate gratitude. Thank and notice the positives in your life, thereby creating an attitudinal magnet for more things to be thankful for.

12. Educating and Advocating for Inclusivity:

Nick emerged as a strong advocate of inclusiveness and equal chances. His work goes beyond his individual successes to promote a world where everyone is accepted for who they are.

Lesson: Promote inclusiveness and equanimity. Utilize your own experiences and voice to help in the creation of a more inclusive and compassionate world.

13. Inspiring self-reflection:

Nick's story makes people contemplate their own lives, hardships, and desires. It stimulates self-analysis, which makes people wonder about themselves.

The Positive Thinking Blueprint

The life of Nick Vujicic serves as an example of how to develop a positive thinking mindset—a mindset that rises above limitations, embraces positive energy, and confronts challenges with resilience. As we look back on the ideas that we get from his amazing life, we realize that this is an example of not only inspiration but also a practical way of living our own lives.

The story of Nick's life experience contains threads of positivity, resilience, adaptability, and the incessant longing for self-improvement. His story forces us to re-evaluate what we see, face up to our self-imposed restrictions, and realize the huge potential that lies within us.

Nick's journey can therefore be summed up as a transformative journey. It is an action call—to take on challenges, develop a positive attitude, and grow beyond known limits. The chapters of this book are laid out as a map, leading one through the complexities of personal development, purposeful living, and a free life.

The legacy of Nick Vujicic resonates through the text, reinforcing the fact that the positive thinking paradigm is not a mere theory but rather a lived reality. It is the power to select optimism, meet difficulties with fortitude, and live a life of perpetual growth and service.

Lessons Learned: Nick's tale is a great example of how a positive mindset doesn't involve rejecting difficulties but rather taking them with determination and appreciation. Through concentrating on things that were in his power and turning obstacles into opportunities, Nick not only changed his life but also became a role model for thousands of other people.

Connection and Relatability: The story of Nick is inspirational because it is based on core concepts such as victory over difficulties, self-contentment, and the influence of a positive mindset. His way makes us feel connected by demonstrating that, under all circumstances, having a positive outlook can bring about deep and profound change.

"In other words, if I lose, I try again and again and again." Nick Vujicic

Welcome to "The Positive Thinking Mindset," a journey of empowerment, resilience, and the unlimited opportunities that follow when we accept the remarkable force of our minds.

As you read further, "The Positive Thinking Mindset" turns into a process of change. The power of Nick Vujicic's strength does not come from his words but rather from the profound wisdom his resilience inspired, and this guide aims to be more than just words on paper; it strives to be the catalyst for profound change in your life.

Come with me on a journey of positivity, where each chapter is an unlocking of potential. Imagine a life in which problems are ladders and failures are the beginnings of success. When you get inside what positive thinking is all about, you are not simply reading a book but getting an entry into a mentality that can refurbish your world.

Here's what awaits you:

1. Unleashing Inner Strength: Find the stores of power in you that are there to be discovered. Discover how difficulties turn into favorable moments and impediments into steps of progress.

2. Building Resilience: Sail through the troubles of life with new-found strength. Learn from the incredibly inspirational journey of Nick Vujicic and prepare yourself to confront all adversities and recover every time stronger.

3. Cultivating Optimism: Acquire the skill of nurturing optimism even when confronted with challenges. Cultivate a positive mindset that not only changes your view of challenges but also brings positive vibes into your life.

4. Fostering Self-Discovery: Start a quest of self-realization, uncovering your weaknesses and strengths, as well as the boundless potential that dwells in you. As a guide, this book shows you how to release who you really are.

5. Creating a Positive Ripple Effect: As you absorb the teachings in these pages, observe how positivity straight from the teachings starts to reflect in your relationships, work, and every single corner of your life. Be a source of motivation and an example for others.

While turning the pages of "The Positive Thinking Mindset," picture a life where each day is a canvas that needs the strokes of your positive thinking to make it a masterpiece. This is not a mere book, but a blueprint for a more enlightened and self-empowered future.

On this transformative journey, are you ready to go? Your copy is waiting for you to change again—not just read, but a profound experience that might reinvent your life. **Let the voyage begin.**

This is the sixth book of the " **Ultimate Mindset Mastery Series**". You can check out the other five books, below:

[Click here to learn more about the **Ultimate Mindset Mastery Series**](#)

Check out the Ultimate Mindset Mastery Series

Or

*Scan this QR Code with your smart
phone to check out the Ultimate
Mindset Mastery Series.*

CHAPTER TWO

UNDERSTANDING THE POWER OF POSITIVE THINKING

THE SILVER LINING

I NEVER REALIZED ONE small act could alter the path of my life until I missed the train. Standing on the platform when my ride left, that morning, frustration washed over me, and I was anxious that my day would become a cloud of frustration. How little did I know that this minor disappointment would be the start of a major change in my attitude.

While I was there, trying to figure out what should I do, a stranger came up to me. He was Sam, a passenger whom you would also think held on to life. Instead of complaining about the lost train, he smiled and said, "Life is full of surprises."

His words resonated with me, and at that point, I decided to look at this failure as a blessing rather than an obstacle. As we chatted over coffee, I noticed how lovely it was to surrender to the unanticipated.

For couple of weeks Sam and I kept on with our morning cup of coffee. All the trains that were missed are actually opportunities to find hidden treasures of the city, meet interesting new people, and engage in a conversation that broadens my horizons. It had seemed that the whole world was determined to prove me that every cloud has silver lining.

Walking through a neighborhood I was unfamiliar with, my friend and I one day found a community garden. I came to life thanks to the gay colors of sweetly blooming flowers and the fragrant earth. This was all in stark contrast to the hurried routine of catching trains and dodging crowds.

Spurred by this respect for the unpredictable, I resolved to help out in the community garden. Watering plants and recovering with other volunteers was a source of satisfaction greater than a routine. The thought dawned on me that my optimistic outlook had made way to opportunities which I had never thought of before.

Later on, I started facing difficulties with another approach. Rather than dwell on failures, I found something good in every circumstance. Unforeseen and unwanted turns of life turned into a source of development, knowledge and contacts.

The power of my positive attitude did not just drive change in my life but also through my surroundings.

As I look back on that lost train and the accidental encounter with Sam, I am thankful for the change in the viewpoint. A simple mind shift that started grew into a journey of self-awareness, community and passion for life. In the end it appears that deep changes can occur from the minor changes of thinking.

So there I stand, open to the beauty of the unlikely, curious about the odyssey, and thanks for the trains that I missed as they have given me a life full of silver lining.

The story here highlights several key aspects of the importance of a positive mindset and its impact on mental well-being:

1. Resilience in the Face of Setbacks:

I suffered the first disappointment of no-train, a situation that is normally an annoying one.

Rather than focus on the disappointment, I viewed it as an unexpected opportunity. This "never say die" approach is a key feature of positive mental attitude.

2. Embracing the Unexpected:

The accidental meeting with Sam and the choice of the tour of the city instead of catching the train symbolize openness to the surprises.

A positive attitude leads to tolerance of new opportunities and the belief in the capacity of development in unexpected circumstances. It prompts people to leave the familiarity zone and walk into the unknown.

3.Finding Joy in Simple Pleasures:

The community garden had the power to make me feel great and satisfied. Optimistic attitude helps people to find happiness in small everyday things. It changes the orientation from what might be missing to the beauty of the now.

4. Opportunities for Growth and Learning:

Participating in the community garden volunteer program led to an unplanned path of individual and community development.

The optimistic approach perceives challenges as a form of learning and growth. It makes people see that failures are not obstacles but are building stones for individual and collective development.

5.Influence on Interactions and Relationships:

Where two positive spirits come together, they are contagious to others though their activities.

Positivity is contagious. A good attitude can improve the relationships allowing them to become supportive and encouraging. Sam's view impacted others who in turn produced the ripple of positive wave.

6.**Gratitude and Appreciation**: I have fallen in love with the community garden and colours of the life. Appreciation is a basis of an affirmative attitude. It is about perceiving and valuing the uplifting things in life which contributes to satisfaction and happiness.

Concept and its Impact on Mental Well-Being:

The story exemplifies how a positive mindset can profoundly impact mental well-being:

1.Shift in Perspective: Positive thinking is a change of conscious attitude. The decision to regard setbacks as opportunities resulted in the change in my mindset and this led to more resilience and flexibility.

2.Reduced Stress and Anxiety: My choice to welcome the surprises and delights of the little things helped to cut down stresses and anxieties. Positive attitude promotes concentration in what can be done and leaving what could not be done.

3.Sense of Fulfillment: Participating in activities that were sources of happiness and satisfaction, for example volunteering in the neighborhood garden, probably added to the general feeling of welfare. A positive attitude looks for satisfaction above the outward conditions.

4.Social Connection and Support: Having a positive attitude helped me to influence my relationships with others enabling a positive social network. To be mentally healthy, constructive relationships are indispensable.

The story above illustrates the perception that the positivity of the thought will be able to help in facing challenges in a person's life, elevating personal growth and promoting the benefits of mental health. The story reflects as a true spirit to the powerful influence of the acceptance of positive feedback even amidst troubling circumstances.

Scientific and psychological perspectives on the advantages of positive thinking.

However, being positive is more than just a short-lived feeling; it is a state of mind which determines our life. An article appeared in the "Journal of Personality and Social Psychology" report presenting that optimistic people live longer and enjoy better health. The force of positive thought is not only the improvement of mental health but also impact the condition of physical wellness.

1.Neuroscientific Perspective: Neuroscience enlightens on the repercussions of positive thoughts for the human brain. A number of studies were done by Dr. Richard J. Davidson, a prominent neuroscientist, to probe into the brain's plasticity and the way positive thinking reshapes the neural pathways. The findings are presented in the book "The Emotional Life of Your Brain," and the key focus is the flexibility of the brain and its ability to react to positive thoughts.Health Benefits: Positive attitude to life manifests in physical health. A research made by the American Heart Association established that people with an optimistic outlook of life have the lowest risk of heart disease and stroke. The research, which is cross-sectional in nature and which uses long-term analysis of the participants, substantiates the association between positive affect and cardiovascular health.

2.**Psychological Resilience**: Resilience as a psychological characteristic is also the ability to rise above the negative impact of life which is part of positive thinking. Dr. Martin Seligman, sometimes identified as the father of positive psychology, has a lot of research done about learned optimism. The book "Learned Optimism" outlines his work and explains how individuals can develop a sturdy state of mind by thinking positively.

3.**Social Impact**: Positive thinking is much more than an element of personal welfare, it affects intercommunication and relationships. The Harvard Study of Adult Development, one of the longest studies of adult life, found that happy relationships were the most important factor in happiness and overall life satisfaction. Fostering the positive thoughts is a part of development the associations.

4.**Productivity and Success**: The correlation of optimism and career achievement is demonstrated by numerous researches. A meta-analysis of positivity and job performance studies was carried out by researchers from the University of Pennsylvania and University of Michigan. The research, which is published in the Journal of Organizational Behavior, discloses a positive association between optimistic attitude and successful career.

5.**Cultural and Philosophical Insights**: Positive thinking goes beyond the results of science; it is derived from cultural and philosophical sources. Ideas of positive thinking are echoed in the philosophies of antiquity such as Stoicism and Buddhism. The stoic focus on the things that are in our power coincides with one of the main principles of positive thinking in which people are supposed to direct their strength on constructive thoughts.

6.**Practical Strategies:** Implementation of positive thinking in everyday life needs practical approaches. The Mayo Clinic as a respected medical establishment offers useful recommendations on how to keep a positive mind. They include gratitude practice, connection with beloved ones, and activities that make you happy.

Positive thinking mastery should be approached from a comprehensive point of view, considering its effects on mind, body, and social relations. Substantial and relevant literature and sources substantiate the cathartic potential of positive thinking turning it into a topic of great substance and relevance. Let's focus on some of the activities that we can use to embrace positivity in our lives.

1.Enhanced Mental Health:

Many studies indicate that having a positive attitude is linked to low stress levels, anxiety and depression.Positive thinking will lead to better mental health through creation of resilience and coping mechanisms in difficult periods.

2.Physical Health Benefits:

Positive attitude is associated with some positive physical health outcomes such as improve immunity, lower blood pressure, and less chronic diseases.

Positive people are likely to practice healthier activities, including healthy eating and regular physical exercises, which promote general well-being.

3.Increased Resilience:

24

Research indicates that people that are in optimistic frame of mind are typically more resilient under stress.

Optimistic attitude helps people to make a situation into an opportunity for growth, thus, increasing their resilience.

4.Improved Coping Mechanisms:

Positive thinking is linked to more efficient ways of coping with stressors.

Positive people are prone to use problem-solving and positive reappraisal techniques in dealing with challenges, hence, achieving better psychological results.

5.Longevity and Health span:

According to some studies, positive-thinking is related to longevity such that a positive person may live longer.A positive attitude leads a person to live a better life, less damaging stress, and better health, which makes the health and life longer and healthier.

6.Enhanced Social Connections:

Positive people mostly attract positive social environment and support, which helps them to have a positive state of being.

Positive thinking leads to stronger relationships because positive people generally bring warmth, empathy and a focus on shared positive experiences in their interaction.

7.Cognitive Benefits:

Optimism has been linked to better cognitive functioning and lower risk of cognitive deterioration in the elderly.

A good attitude may improve cognitive functions, that is, problem solving, creativity and decisiveness.

8. Heart Health:

Some studies suggest that optimistic people have a lower incidence of cardiovascular diseases. Positive thoughts are associated with healthier actions, less stress and lower inflammation, leading to a healthier heart.

9. Workplace Benefits:

Positive thinking is linked to higher job satisfaction, productivity, and success in the work place.

A positive attitude creates a more conducive and teamwork-oriented working atmosphere that ultimately leads to success for the individual and the organization.

Once the benefits of positive attitude are clear, let's get to know where to start.

Here's a guide with practical suggestions and coping mechanisms:

1.Gratitude Journaling:

Tip: Begin a gratitude journal that you will write at least three things you are grateful for on a daily basis.

Actionable Step: Carve out a few minutes in the evening for positivity inventory: contemplate the highlights of the day and record them.

Mindfulness Meditation:

Tip: Introduce mindfulness meditation in your daily schedule to stay here and now and free of stress.

Actionable Step: Start with short practices, paying attention to your breath and increase the time when you are ready.

2.Positive Affirmations:

Tip: Create affirmations that are directed at the goals and self-worth, and are positive, empowering and feel good.

Actionable Step: Say these affirmations every day, especially in self-doubt or challenging situations.

3.Visualization Techniques:

Tip: Picture your goals and how you will proceed to reach them. Actionable Step: Develop a picture of success and come back to it frequently for inspiration.

Challenge Negative Thoughts:

Tip: Reframe negative thoughts and question their truth.

Actionable Step: In an event of a negative thought, one should ask whether there is any evidence to support it and think of an alternative, more positive angle.

4.Surround Yourself with Positivity:

Tip: Pick positive influences in your circle of friends and minimize exposure to negativities.

Actionable Step: Be involved in activities and associate with people who make you feel good about yourself.

5.Practice Self-Compassion:

Tip: Be kind and patient with yourself, especially in the difficult moments.

Actionable Step: In the face of obstacles, talk to yourself in the same way you would to a friend, giving words of encouragement.

6.Set Realistic Goals:

Tip: Chunk larger goals into smaller doable steps.

Actionable Step: Celebrate minor successes in the middle of the road, consolidating the positive attitude by the feeling of achievement.

7.Engage in Positive Hobbies:

Tip: Take a look at the activities which bring you joy and creativity.

Actionable Step: Allocate some scheduled time for activities owned by you that bring happiness.

8.Connect with Positive Communities:

Tip: Participate in groups or communities that have the same interests and encourage positivity.

Actionable Step: Partake in the talks, exchange ideas, and get motivated by kindred spirits.

10.Practice Acts of Kindness:

Tip: Do some acts of kindness for strangers selflessly.

Actionable Step: Practice acts of goodness in your daily routine, which creates a beneficial effect on both you and others.

11.Continuous Learning and Growth:

Tip: Accept there is always a time and space for learning and development.

Actionable Step: Allocate time for reading, attending workshops, or enrolling in courses which are relevant to your interests and objectives.

12.Limit Media Exposure:

Tip: Be careful about what you watch on media.

Actionable Step: Limit the intake of negative news and focus on content that enlightens and informs in a positive way.

13.Celebrate Progress:

Tip: Recognize and enjoy your small victories.

Actionable Step: Assess your accomplishments often and be grateful for the path.

14.Seek Support:

Tip: Seek support from friends, relative, or a mental health professional as necessary.

Actionable Step: Create a support system and be open about your feelings and struggles. Let readers make these tips their own by adding them to their lifestyle and individual preferences. Consistency and step-wise implementation are essential in nurturing the positive attitude over the course of time.

Summary of key take aways

The story is about a man who missed his train and meets another passenger named Sam. By their interaction, he learns the value of welcoming the unexpected turns of the life. This change of view makes him realize the importance of the cherishing the small pleasures of life and the essential role of the positive attitude in keeping the mental sanity.

Positive thinking develops such features as gratefulness, and also self-development. It also promotes the wellbeing, and adaptability. Additionally, it improves the cognitive skills, decreases the danger of cardiovascular diseases and also success in a career.

By using different methods, the people can develop a positive attitude. The other activities are being grateful through journal writing, mindfulness through meditation, positive sayings through affirmations, thinking positively through visualization, proactive self-love, goal setting, empowering hobbies, building supportive networks, and seeking help.

CHAPTER THREE

OVERCOMING LIMITING BELIEFS

INTEGRATION OF TALENTS

I N THE HEART OF Renaissance Italy, where art, culture, and intellectual fervor flourished, lived a young polymath named Leonardo da Vinci. While revered today as one of the greatest geniuses in history, Leonardo's journey was marked by formidable challenges and self-imposed limitations.

Leonardo's Limiting Belief: As a young artist and inventor, Leonardo harbored a deep-seated belief that his insatiable curiosity and diverse interests were a hindrance rather than an asset. He felt torn between his passion for painting, engineering, anatomy, and countless other pursuits. This internal conflict led him to perceive his polymathic nature as a limitation, slowing down his progress in any specific field.

The Turning Point: The turning point in Leonardo's life came when he encountered a mentor who recognized the brilliance within him. Verrocchio, a prominent artist and sculptor, saw beyond the self-doubt that plagued Leonardo. Verrocchio encouraged him to embrace his multifaceted talents rather than viewing them as a hindrance. It was under Verrocchio's guidance that Leonardo began to see the synergy between his various interests.

Overcoming Self-Doubt: Leonardo's journey to overcome self-doubt was not instantaneous. It required a deep introspection into his own thought patterns and a conscious effort to challenge the limiting beliefs that held him back. He started to view his diverse skills not as a weakness but as a unique strength that set him apart.

Integration of Talents: Instead of compartmentalizing his skills, Leonardo began integrating them. His anatomical studies informed his art, and his engineering prowess enriched his inventions. The Vitruvian Man, one of his iconic works, beautifully exemplifies this integration, showcasing the harmony between art and science. By embracing the interconnectedness of his abilities, Leonardo transcended the confines of limiting beliefs.

Unprecedented Achievements: Freed from the shackles of self-doubt, Leonardo's creativity soared to new heights. His notebooks, filled with sketches, observations, and ideas, became a testament to the boundless possibilities of a mind unleashed from limiting beliefs. The Mona Lisa, The Last Supper, and his groundbreaking engineering designs stand as enduring symbols of a Renaissance man who defied constraints.

Legacy of Triumph: Leonardo da Vinci's triumph over limiting beliefs left an indelible mark on history. His legacy extends beyond his individual achievements; it serves as a beacon for those grappling with self-doubt and internal barriers. Leonardo's story teaches us that embracing our multifaceted nature and breaking free from limiting beliefs can lead to unparalleled innovation and creativity.

Lets take a look at another example.

Let's explore the story of Thomas Edison, a prolific inventor whose journey was marked by perseverance and a relentless pursuit of innovation, overcoming his own set of limiting beliefs.

1. Early Challenges and Learning Style: Thomas Edison faced considerable challenges during his early years. His teachers considered him a slow learner, and he was deemed unfit for traditional schooling. Edison's limiting belief, instilled by societal norms, was that academic success was the sole measure of intelligence. However, he overcame this by recognizing his unique learning style and pursuing self-directed learning.

2. Embracing Failure as Progress: Edison's journey as an inventor was riddled with failures. His attempts to invent the electric light bulb encountered numerous setbacks. Instead of viewing these failures as obstacles, Edison saw them as valuable lessons. He famously remarked, "I have not failed. I've just found 10,000 ways that won't work." Edison's ability to reframe failure as an integral part of the learning process enabled him to overcome the limiting belief that setbacks equate to personal inadequacy.

3. Persistence in the Face of Criticism: Edison faced scepticism and criticism from contemporaries who doubted the feasibility of his inventions. His belief in the potential of his ideas allowed him to persist despite external doubts. Overcoming the limiting belief that one must conform to conventional wisdom, Edison forged ahead with his innovative pursuits, eventually earning recognition for his groundbreaking contributions.

4. Adapting to Changing Circumstances: Edison's foray into electric power generation faced challenges due to the prevailing direct current (DC) technology. Despite being a proponent of DC initially, he embraced the alternating current (AC) system when it proved more practical. This ability to adapt and evolve challenged the limiting belief that sticking rigidly to one's ideas is a sign of strength.

5. Team Collaboration and Leadership: Edison surrounded himself with a team of skilled individuals, recognizing that collaboration enhances creativity. This approach was a departure from the limiting belief that a single genius must shoulder the burden of innovation. Edison's leadership style involved inspiring and guiding a team, fostering an environment where diverse talents could thrive.

6. Impact on Modern Society: Edison's breakthroughs, including the electric light bulb and the phonograph, revolutionized modern society. His ability to overcome limiting beliefs extended beyond personal challenges to societal norms. Edison's innovations challenged the status quo, demonstrating that unconventional thinking could lead to transformative change.

7. Legacy of Innovation and Entrepreneurship: Edison's legacy is not just in the numerous patents he held but, in the paradigm, shift he brought to innovation and entrepreneurship. His story teaches us that overcoming limiting beliefs often involves challenging established norms and persistently pursuing one's vision, even in the face of adversity.

Thomas Edison's journey is a proof to the power of persistence, adaptability, and a mindset that views failure as a stepping stone to success. By overcoming societal expectations, embracing failure, and fostering collaborative innovation, Edison left an indelible mark on the world and reshaped the way we perceive inventors and innovators.

Recent research has shed light on effective strategies to tackle and transcend these self-imposed restrictions.

One notable area of study revolves around the concept of cognitive restructuring. Cognitive restructuring involves identifying and challenging negative thought patterns that contribute to limiting beliefs. Research, such as that conducted by Dr. Aaron Beck and his cognitive therapy approach, emphasizes the importance of examining and changing distorted thinking.

Another avenue of exploration centres on the impact of mindset. Stanford psychologist Carol Dweck has extensively studied the concept of fixed versus growth mindsets. Her research suggests that individuals with a growth mindset, who believe their abilities can be developed through dedication and hard work, are more likely to overcome limiting beliefs than those with a fixed mindset.

Neuroscience has also contributed valuable insights. Brain imaging studies have demonstrated that our brains exhibit neuroplasticity, the ability to reorganize and form new neural connections throughout life. This means that with deliberate effort and practice, individuals can rewire their brains, challenging and altering deeply ingrained limiting beliefs.

Furthermore, research in positive psychology has explored the impact of gratitude and positive affirmations. Expressing gratitude has been linked to increased well-being and a more positive outlook on life. Similarly, repeating positive affirmations can reframe negative thought patterns, fostering a more optimistic mindset.

Social psychology studies highlight the influence of social support on belief systems. Having a supportive network can significantly impact one's ability to overcome limiting beliefs. Research by psychologists like Albert Bandura emphasizes the role of social modeling, where observing others successfully navigate challenges can inspire confidence and belief in one's own capabilities.

It's important to note that while these research findings offer valuable insights, the effectiveness of overcoming limiting beliefs often depends on individual factors. Personalized approaches, combining various strategies based on an individual's unique circumstances, may yield the best results.

Recent research findings suggest that a combination of cognitive restructuring, cultivating a growth mindset, leveraging neuroplasticity, practicing gratitude and positive affirmations, and fostering social support can contribute to overcoming limiting beliefs. These strategies, when tailored to individual needs, empower individuals, to break free from self-imposed constraints and reach new heights.

Now let's take a look at how to identify and challenge, some of the self-limiting beliefs. Identifying and challenging self-limiting beliefs is a crucial step towards personal growth and achieving one's full potential.

Here are some practical steps to help you recognize and overcome these limiting beliefs:

1. Self-Awareness:

Start by developing a heightened sense of self-awareness. Pay attention to your thoughts and emotions, especially in challenging situations.

Notice recurring patterns of negative self-talk or thoughts that undermine your confidence or potential.

2. Question Your Beliefs and Identify Negative Thoughts:

Actively question the beliefs that make you feel limited. Ask yourself where these beliefs originated and whether they are based on facts or assumptions.

Challenge the evidence supporting these beliefs. Are there real-life instances that prove these beliefs wrong?

Start by becoming aware of negative thoughts as they arise. Pay attention to your inner dialogue and recognize when you're engaging in self-critical or pessimistic thinking.

Actively question the validity of your negative thoughts. Ask yourself if there is concrete evidence supporting these thoughts or if they are based on assumptions or irrational fears.

3. Seek Feedback:

Reach out to friends, mentors, or colleagues for constructive feedback. Sometimes, others can provide valuable insights that challenge your self-limiting beliefs.

Ask for specific examples where your perceived limitations may not align with how others see your capabilities.

4. Identify Triggers:

Pay attention to situations or environments that trigger self-limiting beliefs. Understanding the specific triggers can help you anticipate and address these beliefs proactively.

Consider keeping a journal to track instances where you felt limited and the thoughts associated with those situations.

5. Replace Negative Thoughts and Cognitive Restructuring:

Once you identify a self-limiting belief, consciously replace it with a positive and empowering thought. Replace negative thoughts with realistic ones. For example, if you catch yourself thinking, "I can't do this," replace it with "I may face challenges, but I can learn and improve with effort.

6. Use Affirmations:

Use positive affirmations that challenge and counteract negative beliefs. Repeat positive statements regularly to reinforce a more empowering mindset.

These are concise, positive statements that reflect the reality you want to create. Repeat them regularly to reinforce a more optimistic mindset.

6. Set Realistic Goals:

Break down larger goals into smaller, achievable steps. This not only makes your objectives more manageable but also helps build confidence along the way.

Celebrate small victories to reinforce a positive mindset and counteract the tendency to focus solely on perceived failures.

7. Mindfulness Meditation:

Practice mindfulness to observe your thoughts without judgment. Mindfulness meditation can help you detach from negative thoughts, allowing you to view them more objectively and prevent them from spiraling into negative emotions.

8. Visualize Success or Positive Visualization:

Visualize positive outcomes and successful scenarios. Imagine yourself overcoming challenges and achieving your goals. Engage your senses to make the visualization more vivid and emotionally impactful.

Use visualization techniques to imagine yourself succeeding in various situations. Visualization can help rewire your brain and create a more positive and confident mental image.

Engage all your senses in the visualization process to make the experience more vivid and impactful.

9. Reframe Catastrophizing:

If your negative thoughts involve catastrophic thinking (assuming the worst-case scenario), challenge these extreme thoughts. Consider alternative, more realistic outcomes and assess the likelihood of each scenario.

10. Thought Records or Journals:

Keep a thought journal where you document negative thoughts, the situations triggering them, and your emotions. This practice helps you identify patterns and provides a foundation for challenging and reframing these thoughts.

11. Challenge Comparisons:

Avoid comparing yourself to others, as this often leads to feelings of inadequacy. Remember that everyone has their unique strengths and challenges.

Focus on your progress and growth rather than measuring yourself against external standards.

12. Continuous Learning:

Embrace a growth mindset, where you view challenges as opportunities to learn and improve. Understand that abilities can be developed through dedication and effort.

Cultivate a habit of continuous learning, seeking new experiences, and embracing challenges that expand your skills and knowledge.

13. Seek Professional Support:

If self-limiting beliefs persist and significantly impact your well-being, consider seeking support from a therapist or a coach. They can provide guidance, tools, and strategies to help you overcome deep-seated beliefs.

Remember, challenging self-limiting beliefs is an ongoing process. By incorporating these steps into your daily life, you can foster a mindset that empowers you to reach new heights and realize your true potential.

By consciously altering the way you think, you can promote a more positive and constructive mindset. Lets also understand that there are several techniques to help you reframe negative thoughts:

14. Gratitude Practice:

Cultivate a habit of gratitude by focusing on positive aspects of your life. Regularly acknowledge and appreciate the good things, no matter how small. This practice shifts your focus from what's lacking to what you have.

15. Learn from Setbacks:

Reframe setbacks as opportunities for learning and growth. Instead of viewing them as failures, consider them stepping stones toward improvement. Ask yourself what lessons you can extract from the experience.

16. Constructive Self-Talk:

Pay attention to your internal dialogue and replace self-critical statements with constructive and compassionate self-talk. Treat yourself with the same kindness and encouragement you would offer a friend.

17. Challenge Perfectionism:

Reframe the belief that everything must be perfect. Embrace the idea that mistakes and imperfections are part of the learning process. Focus on progress rather than aiming for flawless outcomes.

Remember that reframing negative thoughts is a skill that improves with practice. Consistency and patience are key as you incorporate these techniques into your daily life. Over time, you'll likely find that you're better equipped to maintain a more positive and resilient mindset.

Summary of key takeaways: -

Leonardo da Vinci, a Renaissance Italian polymath, faced self-imposed limitations and challenges in his pursuits. His diverse interests, including painting, engineering, and anatomy, led him to view his polymathic nature as a hindrance rather than an asset. However, a mentor named Verrocchio encouraged him to embrace his talents and overcome self-doubt. Leonardo integrated his diverse skills, integrating his anatomical studies and engineering prowess into his art.

This approach allowed him to transcend limiting beliefs and achieve unprecedented achievements, such as the Mona Lisa and The Last Supper. His legacy serves as a beacon for those struggling with self-doubt and internal barriers, demonstrating that embracing one's multifaceted nature can lead to unparalleled innovation and creativity.

Thomas Edison, a prolific inventor, faced numerous challenges and limiting beliefs throughout his life. He recognized his unique learning style and pursued self-directed learning, embracing failure as progress. Despite facing criticism, Edison persevered with his innovative pursuits, eventually earning recognition for his groundbreaking contributions.He adapted to changing circumstances, embracing the alternating current system when it proved more practical. His leadership style involved inspiring and guiding a team, fostering an environment where diverse talents could thrive.

Edison's breakthroughs, including the electric light bulb and the phonograph, revolutionized modern society, challenging the status quo and demonstrating that unconventional thinking could lead to transformative change. His legacy is not just in the numerous patents he held but also in the paradigm shift he brought to innovation and entrepreneurship.

Recent research has explored strategies to overcome limiting beliefs, such as cognitive restructuring, cultivating a growth mindset, leveraging neuroplasticity, practicing gratitude and positive affirmations, and fostering social support. These strategies empower individuals to break free from self-imposed constraints and reach new heights. However, the effectiveness of overcoming limiting beliefs often depends on individual factors, and personalized approaches, combining various strategies based on an individual's unique circumstances, may yield the best results.

Identifying and challenging self-limiting beliefs is a crucial step towards personal growth and achieving one's full potential. To do this, develop self-awareness, question your beliefs, seek feedback, identify triggers, replace negative thoughts with positive ones, use affirmations, set realistic goals, practice mindfulness meditation, visualize success or positive visualization, reframe catastrophic thinking, keep a thought journal, challenge comparisons, embrace continuous learning, and seek professional support.

To reframe negative thoughts, cultivate gratitude practices, learn from setbacks, use constructive self-talk, and challenge perfectionism. Focus on the positive aspects of your life and acknowledge and appreciate the good things in your life. Learn from setbacks as opportunities for learning and growth, treating them as stepping stones toward improvement. Pay attention to your internal dialogue and replace self-critical statements with constructive and compassionate self-talk.

Remember that reframing negative thoughts is an ongoing process and requires consistency and patience. By incorporating these techniques into your daily life, you can foster a mindset that empowers you to reach new heights and realize your true potential. Techniques to help you reframe negative thoughts include gratitude practice, learning from setbacks, constructive self-talk, and challenging perfectionism. Consistency and patience are key as you incorporate these techniques into your daily life, and over time, you'll likely find yourself better equipped to maintain a more positive and resilient mindset.

CHAPTER FOUR

THE GROWTH MINDSET MENTALITY

SHIFT YOUR PERSPECTIVE

S INCE MY CHILDHOOD, I used to look up to my grandfather. He was a wise man, a man of force and boundless quest. His manner of living was interesting, as a child, I admired his way of dealing with issues smoothly and successfully. One particular incident is etched in my memory, an incident that had a profound impact on me and culminated into my perception of the mindset of growth.

The sun was shining, and I was working with my grandfather on his garden. As we got busy together, he related stories of his own upbringing, emphasizing the significance of fortitude and an optimistic outlook. He shared with me the challenges he experienced while growing up in a small village, the barriers he had broken, and the teachings that life had taught him.

However, it was not only his words but also his conduct that stuck to me. Though my grandfather had lived through a lot of obstacles, he always dealt with them by an unshakeable faith in his ability to learn and evolve. Be it learning a new skill, dealing with complicated relationships, or adjusting to change, he viewed all of them as learning experiences.

The man's love and devotion towards his garden also opened my eyes to the fact that such principles were applicable throughout all facets of life. We could also be like the plants in his garden and become healthy and happy if we have the proper level of thinking. Both my grandfather's upbringing and personal life events shape his journey toward having a growth mindset. Being born in a poor family in a small village, he encountered a lot of difficulties from the very beginning. Yet, rather than giving in to calamity, he decided to live with an attitude of survival, which is the core of flexibility, adaptability, and craving for knowledge.

Another significant factor in his progress was the factors of his very family. During his growing years, he watched his parents and elder brothers and sisters maneuver through tough situations with strong will and beauty. Their determination in the efficacy of hard work and education had a major influence on him, being a cornerstone of his growth-mindset mentality.

My grandfather had many misfortunes throughout his life - from financial problems to personal losses. However, with every challenge, he decided to see prospect instead of failure. He did not see defeats as marks of ineptitude rather as worthwhile lessons to be learnt about from which he will draw his development.

One of the defining moments in his life happened during his youth when he opted to continue his studies despite the fact that his finances were limited. Even though others were sceptical and discouraged him, he was unwavering that education holds the future. By dint of determination and perseverance, he got scholarships, held part-time jobs, and finally graduated with honors.

It was such an unceasing search for knowledge and self-development that formed his growth mentality. He realized that intelligence and skill were not fixed attributes but that they could be cultivated with hard work and determination. He turned every challenge into a learning experience and never let failures stop him.

Following the life path of my grandfather, I couldn't but become amazed by his courage and persistency. His case showed me that success is not rooted in situation but in attitudes. I discovered that failures are not defeats but chance to grow, and real victory comes from taking up challenges and not running away from them.

His stories and his actions gave me priceless lessons that have directed me through my life. I gained the understanding of the perseverance in the time of difficulties, the impact of the attitude and continuous learning and development.

The legacy of my grandfather continues to motivate me even now. When I encounter difficulties or failures, I reflect on what he told me and how he lived. I try to represent the similar spirit of flexibility and development, realizing that with the proper attitude, everything is achievable.

In other words, my grandfather's path to the formation of a growth mindset is a clear example of how belief, determination, and lifelong learning can change a life. Not only has his life story dictated my own outlook but it has also left me with a profound respect for the endless possibilities that lie within each of us.

With time, I have realised that the growth mindset approach is not innate but it is nurtured through our experiences and choices. It is also an attitude that failure is a path to success and that we are capable of learning and growing.

From my grandfather's example, I have known that setbacks are not obstacles but rather turnings on the road of success. The positive attitude and readiness to learn help to conquer life challenges that seem to be insurmountable and attain our objectives.

Memories of my grandfather's lessons have been with me all through my life, providing the necessary guidance in times of joy and sorrow. They have provided me with the concept of sustainability, the might of optimism and the notion of lifelong learning.

In fact, how the growth mindset mentality is developed is a story of determination, faith and an unyielding will for personal growth. It is an affirmation that have the right attitude, anything can be achieved.

Therefore, as I pursue my own path, I seek to reflect the same sense of resilience and endurance that my grandfather had once taught me. To me, each challenge is a chance to own growth, as I am fully aware that with the right attitude I can triumph over any obstacle that I face.

Ideally, the proper understanding of my life history is that challenges should be embraced and failure should provide lessons if one wishes to grow. I also hold the view that one can overcome obstacles and transform failures into useful learning experiences when certain tips are applied, which are listed in the following paragraphs.

Shift Your Perspective:

According to a study published in the Journal of Personality and Social Psychology, individuals who view challenges as opportunities for growth are more likely to demonstrate resilience and achieve long-term success (Dweck, 2006). Mindset: The New Psychology of Success. Random House.

I remember when as a college graduate, I faced rejection from multiple job applications. Instead of feeling defeated, I viewed each rejection as an opportunity to refine my resume, interview skills, and networking strategies. Eventually, my positive mindset and perseverance paid off when I landed MY dream job at a reputable company.

Tip: Start reframing challenges as opportunities for growth and learning.

Actionable Step: When faced with a setback or obstacle, ask yourself, "What can I learn from this experience?" Focus on the lessons you can extract rather than dwelling on the negative aspects. Instead of viewing challenges as obstacles, see them as opportunities for growth and learning. Embrace them as chances to develop new skills, expand your knowledge, and become stronger.

Set Realistic Goals:

Research conducted by Locke and Latham found that setting specific and challenging goals can significantly enhance performance and motivation (Locke & Latham, 2002).Building a practically useful theory of goal setting and task motivation: A 35-year odyssey. American Psychologist, 57(9), 705–717.

I remember , close friend of mine, Kenneth, had a habit of breaking down his ultimate dream into doable small steps. He, as an aspiring entrepreneur, wanted to start his own business. Rather than setting vague goals like "become successful," he would break down his vision into actionable steps, such as "research target market," "create business plan," and "launch prototype." By setting specific and challenging goals, Kenneth was able to stay focused and motivated on his entrepreneurial journey.

Tip: Break down big goals into smaller, more manageable tasks.

Actionable Step: Create a list of specific actions you need to take to achieve your goal. Set deadlines for each task to keep yourself accountable and track your progress along the way. Break down big challenges into smaller, more manageable goals. This will make them feel less daunting and help you track your progress along the way.

Develop Resilience:

A study published in the Journal of Personality and Social Psychology found that individuals with higher levels of resilience tend to have better mental health outcomes and adapt more effectively to stressful situations (Smith et al., 2008). The Brief Resilience Scale: Assessing the Ability to Bounce Back. International Journal of Behavioral Medicine, 15(3), 194–200.

Recently I read in the community newspaper inspiring details of a high school student, Tina, who initially struggled with academic performance due to a learning disability. Despite facing numerous setbacks, she refused to give up on her education. With the support of her teachers and family, Tina developed resilience by seeking alternative learning strategies, such as tutoring and assistive technology. Eventually, her perseverance paid off when she graduated with honors and was accepted into her top-choice college. Cultivate resilience by building a strong support network of friends, family, mentors, and peers who can provide encouragement and guidance during difficult times.

Tip: Cultivate a growth mindset by viewing setbacks as temporary obstacles and opportunities for growth. Embrace challenges as learning experiences that can strengthen your resilience and adaptability.

Actionable Step: Practice reframing negative thoughts into positive affirmations. When faced with a setback or obstacle, challenge yourself to find at least one positive aspect or lesson to take away from the experience. Write down these affirmations and revisit them regularly to reinforce your resilience mindset.

Practice Self-Compassion:

Research by Neff and Dahm found that practicing self-compassion is associated with lower levels of anxiety, depression, and stress, as well as greater resilience in the face of adversity (Neff & Dahm, 2015). Self-compassion: What it is, what it does, and how it relates to mindfulness. In M. Robinson, B. Meier, & B. Ostafin (Eds.), Mindfulness and Self-Regulation (pp. 121–140). Springer.

I, once, experienced a major setback in my career, when I felt overwhelmed with feelings of self-doubt and inadequacy. Instead of being hard on myself, I practiced self-compassion by acknowledging my emotions and reminding myself that failure is a natural part of the learning process. By treating myself with kindness and understanding, I was able to bounce back stronger and more determined than ever.

Tip: Treat yourself with kindness and understanding, especially during times of failure or difficulty.

Actionable Step: Write yourself a letter of encouragement, highlighting your strengths and acknowledging your efforts. Refer back to it whenever you need a reminder of your worth and capabilities. Be kind to yourself when facing setbacks or failures. Recognize that making mistakes is a natural part of the learning process and treat yourself with the same compassion you would offer to a friend.

Seek Feedback:

According to research published in the Journal of Applied Psychology, feedback-seeking behavior is positively correlated with job performance and career success (Anseel et al., 2015).How Are We Doing After 30 Years? A Meta-Analytic Review of the Antecedents and Outcomes of Feedback-Seeking Behavior. Journal of Management, 41(1), 318–348.

I used to work in one of the marketing firms where there was Tim, a junior employee known for actively seeking feedback from his supervisors about his project presentations. Also, he was responsive to a good critique and would implement advice for improvement with every presentation. So he polished his abilities to communicate with people and started to present even more effective speeches. Consequently, he was noticed by his fellow workers and was promoted in the company.

Tip: Initiate the process of seeking feedback from other people that would assist you to identify blind spots as well as areas for improvement.

Actionable Step: Ask a trusted co-worker, mentor, or supervisor for feedback on the recent project or presentation. Pay close attention and make short notes whenever someone gives their suggestion on growth. Do not hesitate to get feedback from others, it can be a mentor, a colleague or an old friend. Positive criticism is a source of helpful critics, pointing out in what areas you can (or should) improve.

Reflect and Learn:

The Kluger and DeNisi research on meta-analysis demonstrated that reflection and self-evaluation are effective approaches for improving learning and performance (Kluger & DeNisi, 1996). The effects of feedback interventions on performance: Discrete Histories, Meta-Analysis, and Preliminary Feedback Intervention Theory. Psychological Bulletin, 119(2), 254–284.

I worked for a short time at a software development company, and one of the team leaders there, Lisa, introduced weekly reflection sessions with her team so that they could analyse the results of the projects and find areas where the process could be improved. Through open communication and self-reflection, Lisa promoted the spirit of ongoing learning and innovation in her team. Consequently, they were able to rationalize processes, improve efficiency, and produce better products for their customers.

Tip: Carry out reflective sessions on a regular basis to consider your performance and what you have gained from it.

Actionable Step: Allocate time at the end of each week to write in your journal about your experiences, difficulties and achievements. Analyse the positives, the negatives, and the lessons you have got from the experience.

Reflect on your past experiences and discover what worked, what didn't. Failure is a teacher because you will analyse and realize what and where you went wrong and what you can do better next time.

Stay Flexible:

According to the study that was published in the Journal of Organizational Behaviour, flexibility plays an important part in the way people tackle problems. A more flexible approach to the problem makes them more adaptable to the changing circumstances. And more capable as far as problem solving is concerned (De Dreu et al., 2008).

Hedonic Tone and Activation Level in the Mood-creativity Link: The Dual Pathway to Creativity Model. Journal of Organizational Behaviour, 29(7), 835–846.

In a survey conducted by the World Economic Forum, it was found that 86% of the executives argue that adaptability and the ability to respond to change are among the biggest factors of success in the modern workplace (World Economic Forum, 2020). Report of the Future of Jobs 2020.Geneva: World Economic Forum.

One of the marketing managers with whom I had the honour of working for a while was John, who was asked to introduce a range of new products to a very competitive market. Although the implementation had been carefully planned, the unexpected changes of the consumer preferences, and market behaviour were the most crucial factors for launching. Instead of holding on to his initial plan, John showed flexibility and promptly changed his marketing tactic. Remaining adaptive and responsive to the changing terrain John finally managed to launch the products and overachieved the sales targets.

Tip: Accept change and be ready to modify your tactics or approaches.

Actionable Step: Make use of mindfulness practices like deep breathing or meditation to stay in the moment and respond to unknown changes or challenges in a calm manner. Allow yourself to change your methods and to experiment with new techniques in case the things do not go as expected. Flexibility is the cornerstone of being able to conquer obstacles and achieve innovative solutions.

Practice Mindfulness:

In the Journal of Occupational Health Psychology, a study concluded that mindfulness-based interventions are successful when applied in the workplace environment to reduce stress and improve psychological well-being (Shonin et al., 2014).

In a report of the American Psychological Association, it is stated that mindfulness meditation is an effective method of reducing symptoms associated with anxiety, depression, and stress (American Psychological Association,).

I, for instance, have suffered with stress and anxiety throughout my career as a business professional due to the high demands placed upon me. I made up my mind that I would include mindfulness into my daily life. I would meditate for just 10 minutes in the morning before I start my day. With time, I realized that I was getting quieter and balanced, allowing me to be clearer and more focused in approaching the challenges at my work.

John, a college student, in the process of exam preparation, found himself under a great deal of pressure to succeed. He began using the mindfulness practice by taking brief pauses to breathe and centre himself in the present. This made him handle his stress better and deal with his studies with a clearer head.

Tip: Integrate mindfulness practices in your daily life to control stress and anxiety.Actionable Step: Begin with easy mindfulness activities like deep breathing, body scans or mindful walking. Allot a few minutes every day to practice mindfulness and gradually extend the duration as you get more used to it.

Introduce mindfulness methods into your daily life to cope with stress and anxiety. You can use mindfulness to be in the moment and deal with challenges with a clear and focused mind.Focus on Solutions:

Findings by Folkman and Lazarus (1988) published in the Journal of Personality and Social Psychology show that problem-focused coping strategies, which entail focusing on solutions, have strong associations with positive psychological adjustment and resilience in the face of adversity.Gallup survey indicates that people who have a solution-oriented approach rather than dwelling on aspects of the problem have higher levels of life satisfaction and well-being .

In my unremarkable rural area, I remember I met a small business owner who had a cash flow problem that posed a threat for his business to survive. Instead of getting panicked, he sat with his accountant in an attempt to analyse the situation and find possible solutions. They together developed a budgeting plan, renegotiated payment terms with the vendors and initiated a marketing campaign which was aimed at attracting new customers. However, the businessman's action-oriented approach helped him to recover and set his business back on course.

Tip: Change your attention from the problems to finding solutions.

Actionable Step: Divide the problem into tactical and comprehensible chunks. Consider the possible solutions or tricks for each step and rank them regarding their feasibility and influence. Take action decisively to implement the best solutions and modify your approach accordingly. Rather than concentrate on problem, think about the solution. Analyze the problem in chunks and consider other ways to solve it.

Celebrate Progress:

An article in the Journal of Happiness Studies revealed that recognizing and enjoying the accomplishments, however small they may be, is linked with higher levels of happiness and motivation (Mancini & Bonanno).

Amabile and Kramer's research that is discussed in Harvard Business Review shows that organizations that celebrate small victories and milestones have engaged employees and higher productivity levels.

Being a fitness lover, I set the target to run a marathon in a year. To monitor my development, I used to keep a journal where I noted my workouts, goals achieved and personal accomplishments. After setting a new personal record or finishing a hard training session, I used to reward myself with a healthy meal or a new gym clothes. Celebrating my victories as I moved along helped me stay positive and determined in reaching my destination.

Tip: Recognize and honour your successes, small as they may be.

Actionable Step: Create a journal or gratitude jar where you can jot down and keep your moments of accomplishment or progress. Set aside time to review these notes often and be grateful for the progress you have made on your path.

Recognize and rejoice in your success in whatever scale they come. Looking at your success as you move along will increase your self-confidence and love to what you do.

Stay Persistent:

The concept of persistence and grit has been studied by psychologist Angela Duckworth who discovered that individuals who are gritty are more likely to be successful in the long run in various domains such as academics, sport, and career (Duckworth et al.).

According to a survey conducted by the Pew Research Center, those who demonstrated the higher resilience and determination were the one who achieved their long-term goals and aspirations (Pew Research Center).

While I was going home in a train from a trip, I met my high school friend David by sheer coincidence. we had discussions of all kinds of topics. David, spilled the beans on his growth tale. As an upstart business person, he had been turned down several times by investors during his pitch for the business idea. Yet, he did not give up despite the failures. He went on to perfect his pitch, get guidance from mentors, and look into other ways to get finance. All his efforts became effective when he at last got money from a venture capital company and started the business.

Tip: Do not give up from the first sight of failure, instead, persist when afraid.

Actionable Step: Recall your goals and what makes them important to you. Concentrate on the headway you've advanced to date and find motivation in previous achievements to uphold your resolve. Remain strong and move on, knowing that set backs are short lived and every challenge is an opportunity for development.

Be patient and continue forward, because failure is just momentary and sometimes success is a matter of persistence.

Embrace Growth Mindset:

Dweck, a renowned psychologist, has conducted pioneering research which revealed that individuals with a growth mindset who are sure that their abilities can be developed through hard work are more likely to succeed and overcome obstacles.

Fisher et al. in a study published in the Journal of Applied Psychology report that employees with a growth mindset are more likely to look for feedback, learn from failures, and show fortitude at work.

Being a high school student, math was never an easy thing for me and I would often be let down by my poor grades. Assisted by my teacher, I embraced a growth mindset, according to which, I can become better by trying and practicing. I asked for additional assistance, took the tutoring sessions, and solved the difficult exercises until this concept was mastered. Consequently, my grades started to get to be better, and I gained a new assurance in relation to my educational skills.

Tip: Develop a growth mindset by trusting in your capacity to learn and progress with time.

Actionable Step: Question solidified thoughts about your talents and capabilities. Don't take failures as proof of ineptness, but as the means of the growth and learning. Accept challenges with joy, considering that every challenge, no matter how successful or otherwise, helps you grow personally and professionally.

Consider the failures as chances to learn rather than the marks of the failure.W hen following the practical tips and steps, a person will develop a mindset that loves challenges and learns from failures thus ensuring personal and professional transformation. Note that resilience, self-compassion, and a capacity for change are critical elements in overcoming problems and reaching goals.

With such success strategies in place, you become a person who loves to face challenges, learn from failures, and therefore, achieve more satisfaction and fulfillment.

These examples illustrate the ways in which the practical strategies of cultivating a growth-oriented perspective can be implemented in life situations to fight challenges, learn from failures and gain more success. If you practice a growth mindset and apply those strategies to your daily life, you will unleash your full potential and realize success in both personal and professional opportunities.

Summary of Key Take Ways

The author's life has been deeply affected by the growth mindset thinking. It is the belief that, with the right approach, all is possible and obstacles represent opportunities for self-improvement. This type of thought is nurtured through individual experiences and choices rather than being something that is born.

His grandfather family had a strong need for education and hard work, that helped the author to develop a growth mindset. Despite his many failures, he decided to look at them as steps for progress. His determination to pursue education although he was with financial difficulties and met opposites from others, contributed to the strengthening of his belief in the power of education and hard work.

The story of the writer's grandfather is a living example of what faith, perseverance and continuous learning can do. It has made the author realize that one's state of mind, not outside events, defines one's level of success. The author's grandfather has always been a source of inspiration for him all his lives, teaching him about the virtues of dedication, and eternal learning.

We are not born with a growth mindset but rather it is what we create by our experiences and choices. We can conquer the hardest obstacles and achieve our objectives if we perceive problems as opportunities, view defeat as a requisite part of the journey to success, and believe in our ability to develop and transform.

In conclusion, the growth mindset approach acts as a symbol that everything is achievable if one has the right mindset. Living a resilient and determined life, people can solve any situation and reach the final point.

The essay covers a number of methods through which obstacles can be conquered and success in the long term can be gained. It suggests to interpret difficulties as opportunities for learning and development, setting achievable goals, becoming resilient, practicing self-compassion exercises, seeking feedback and focusing on self-reflection.

People can avoid the negative aspects of obstacles by reframing them as opportunities to learn. Progress can also be easily tracked by dividing large objectives into smaller, achievable tasks.

Situational flexibility is one of the major elements of the mental health outcomes. Maintaining a strong social network of colleagues, mentors, family, and friends helps through hardship by providing help and guidance. For elevating your resilience, you should practice rewording negative thoughts into positive affirmations and revisit them as often as possible.

Resilience in the presence of adversity and lower levels of stress, anxiety, and depression are associated with self-compassion, while resilience is practiced. More so in the moments of defeat or hardship, self-love and compassion allow a person to stand up as a stronger and more determined person.

Feedback-seeking behavior is associated with career success and job performance. Identifying blind spots and potential areas of improvement can be facilitated by requesting constructive criticism from a trustworthy colleague, mentor, or supervisor.

Finally, a focus on self-care and self-development will help people to get over various difficulties and achieve long-term success. Adopting these strategies enables individuals to develop a robust mindset, improve mental health, and gain long-term success.

Reflect and learn: Continuous reflective sessions foster open communication and self-evaluation, hence, enhanced learning and performance. This fosters a team-based environment of continuous improvement and learning, thus enhancing productivity and quality of work.

Remain adaptable: The adaptable people can overcome problems and tend to adapt to changes. Accept the change and be ready to alter your goals and methods if the situation requires. Perform mindfulness activities like meditation or deep breathing to stay in the present and respond calmly to unexpected hurdles or change of course.

Begin with simple mindfulness practices such as body scan, mindful walking or deep breathing to assist you in controling stress and anxiety. Introduce mindfulness activities into your everyday life to help you deal with stress and anxiety.

Concentrate on finding solutions: Research has shown that problem-focused coping skills, such as this one, are associated with increased psychological adaptation and resilience during stress. Those who focus on seeking solutions tend to have better general health and higher satisfaction level with life.

Advice: Rather than focusing on problems, start considering the possible solutions. Segment issues into manageable parts and prioritize them based on the degree of their effect and the availability of a solution. Adopt the most potential solutions with enthusiasm, and adjust your approach accordingly.

To conclude, reflective, adaptable, mindful and problem-focused coping skills are crucial in the modern day work environment. Using these strategies, an individual will improve his or her performance, adapt to changing circumstances, and maintain a positive attitude.

Ambitious and success recognition are linked with greater motivation and happiness in addition to higher level of engagement and productivity in businesses. Keep a gratitude jar or diary to write your achievements and read them frequently. Persistence and tenacity are vital to success in many areas, including studies, sports, and professional life.

Development orientation is equally important that is, the idea that people can learn and improve with times. Workers with a growth mindset tend to seek feedback, take responsibility for their mistakes, and be resilient at work. For example, a math-challenged high school student learned to embrace his skills by challenging the stereotype of his potential and talents.

Thanks to the provided useful recommendations and simple to follow exercises, you will acquire the habit to perceive problems as challenges, learn from your errors and become a cheerful and successful person. Surviving challenges in life and triumphing over them at the end demands a great deal of resilience, self-empathy, and flexibility. Through the incorporation of these concepts every individual has a chance to become a significant personality in all spheres of life and in any job.

TAKE A BREAK

WE HAVE REACHED A mid point of the book. You may like to take a break and give a feedback on this book , in the form of a rating or a review on Amazon or Goodreads . This will help immensely in spreading the message in the reading community.

Besides, your suggestions are incredibly important to my creative process as an independent writer. It not only fuels my passion but also allows me to go deeply into the core of my creative attempts and find the very heart of my writing. I respectfully ask that you think about posting a review / rating for " The Positive Thinking Mindset " in order to gain your useful insights and opinions.

It is not necessary for your review to be in-depth or extensive; even a brief collection of ideas that expresses your true feelings will do. Whether your comments are compliments or constructive criticism, they all serve as important building bricks in my search for ongoing development as a writer and storyteller.

You might prefer to scan the QR Code below using your smart phone.

Scan the QR Code with your smart
phone and put a rating or a review

CHAPTER FIVE

THE WEALTH OF WELL BEING

EXPLORING THE CONNECTION BETWEEN

WELL-BEING AND FINANCIAL SUCCESS

WHEN I REFLECT ON my path, it amazes me that once upon a time, I was completely possessed by the chase for having material treasure. I was like the majority of the people who thought that achieving wealth would eventually result in happiness and fulfilment. So, I associated success with money. But it was a string of unanticipated happenings and profound insights that led me to unearth a far more priceless find: the wealth of joy.

Success in the business world was the main aim at the start of my journey. I worked out of ambition but also endangered myself physically and mentally, by working long hours, as I was ambitious and was working to have security in terms of money. Outwardly, I was getting promotions and pay hikes and other trappings of success, but deep within, I was getting emptier and unhappier.

The turning point of my life occurred at the most hectic period at work. I felt tired, anxiety and disillusionment because of the increased pressure and never ending deadlines. My body and mind were telling me that it was the point of no return and that I needed to do something.

One of these catalyst incidents occurred on an especially busy workday. I was in pain due to my efforts to meet tight deadlines and to surpass the expectations of my employer. But I quickly came to understand that my determination to be successful was having an adverse effect on my emotional and psychological well-being. I felt that something had to be done because I was tired, nervous, and stressed.

At that moment of enlightenment, I set the goal to be my health and welfare my priorities. I came to understand that my physical, emotional, and mental health needs to be taken care of before anything else for me to succeed in my professional pursuits. This involved drawing lines, loving myself, and forming practices that fed my body, mind, and spirit.

I found out that real wealth is composed of financial stability and mental coherence, emotional balance, and good health. Having this new awareness, I embarked on a journey of self-awareness and development, aimed at allowing this welfare wealth to flourish in all my aspects.

I started by changing the list of what is more important to me and redefining the success. Rather than running after material possessions and trying to win the approval of others, I concentrated on cultivating real friendships, pursuing my hobbies, and living a minimalistic life. I discovered that real wealth is not found in possessions but rather in manner of life and the influence we have on others.

After that, I began to focus on self-care activities that feed my body, mind, and spirit. I promised to adhere to a regular exercise routine, eat properly, and sleep well since I knew that general well-being mostly relies on physical health. I, too, began to practice mindfulness and meditation as powerful means of stress reduction, gratitude cultivation, and the creation of inner peace.

I spent lots of time and money on lifelong learning and personal development, taking care of my physical and mental health. I searched for coaches and mentors who could lead and support me in my journey to self-knowledge. I was a knowledge addict, who attended seminars and read books in many areas, resilience and emotional intelligence being just a few, learning from experts in various fields.

Having gained knowledge about the diversity of well-being, I started to integrate the ideas of wealth and generosity in my everyday life. I came to understand that the true happiness is not in amassing wealth but in sharing it with others and making the world a better place. I liked helping the needy, and I sent money and time to organizations that had the same views as me.

The lesson of the unity of all dimensions of well-being was one of the deepest teachings of my journeys. I came to know that real wealth includes not only good physical and mental health but also emotional and spiritual satisfaction. I developed significant relationships, forgiveness, compassion, and something bigger than me through nature, art or spiritual practice.

It all began when I realized that true wealth exceeds the limits of material things. Though having money is certainly a necessity, I realized that it can't bring satisfaction and happiness by itself. I came to the understanding that seeking financial achievement demanded me to also develop my psychological and intellectual health and that I had to do both simultaneously.

Changing my definition of success and reprioritizing my goals were two of the first steps I took to achieve this equilibrium. I changed my attention from the external measures such as salary increments or material goods, to personal development and satisfaction. I realized the value of creating significant relationships, working on my dreams, and living in accordance with my beliefs.

Regular exercises were among the areas of self-care I focused on. I came to realize the fact that physical activity played a crucial role in my emotional and psychological status rather than my physical health only. I set some time aside for things that were going to make me relax, re-energize, and become more aware of who I was, such as going for a run in the park or doing a yoga class.

I also took a crucial decision to focus on mindfulness and meditation as a way of reaching balance. I realized the value of mindfulness, living in the here and now, and silencing the chatter in my mind. The habit of my constant meditation helps me to note my thoughts and feelings as they come, and let them go like clouds in the sky without judging them.

A rough day at work was an important lesson that mindfulness can enhance performance. Instead of letting stress overcome me, I breathed deeply and meditated. All this helped me to calm down, clear my head and act with cool.

Investing in myself, I used the books and workshops on resilience, optimism, and emotional intelligence. I situated myself in the centre of mentors who steered and motivated me.A weekend retreat aimed at mindfulness and self-consciousness turned out to be an eureka for myself. It helped me to explore the self and develop my resilience.

Self-care and self-growth focused improved my life on the whole. I was more joyful, in harmony with others, and more immune to hard circumstances.

I have learned not to associate my pleasure with solely the external validation. Instead, I found that the real success is within.

There have been many challenges and failures, but I considered them as opportunities for learning. Considering my career hit a rough patch, I opted to take it as a learning lesson. I returned stronger. Currently, I appreciate a harmonious style of life, which gives priority to self-development, friends, and health.

The more I think about it, I have realized that the true wealth is in living according to my values rather than to possess material riches and accomplishments. I am grateful that today I am where I am and my being is my every day priority.

Here are some practical tips for achieving well-being:

Take care of yourself in the way of exercises, meditation, and enough sleep.

Eat with attention and awareness of the signs from your body.

Train yourself in improving your emotional intelligence.

Cultivate self-awareness by monitoring your feelings and recognizing the thoughts and beliefs underneath.

Engage in emotional regulation practices such as deep breathing, progressive muscle relaxation, and visualization in order to control stress and overwhelm.

Develop empathy and sympathy for yourself and others, knowing that every person goes through difficult times.

1. Manage Stress Effectively:

Stress management techniques including mindfulness meditation, yoga, or tai chi designed to reduce physiological and psychological stress responses, should be used more often.

Develop a supportive environment by setting boundaries, assigning tasks, and asking for help when necessary.

Participate in activities that foster relaxation and stress release like spending time in nature, listening to music or engaging in creative expression.

2. Build Resilience:

Develop a learning mindset by turning the challenges into learning and growing opportunities. Produce positive emotions by concentrating on what you can manipulate and practicing gratitude for the gifts in your life.

Build up coping mechanisms like the ability to think, problem-solving skills, social support networks, and positive self-talk to manage challenges and recover from failures.

3. Nurture Meaningful Relationships:

Make quality more important than quantity in your relationships and spend time and energy developing close and meaningful relationships.

Display active listening and effective communication skills if you want your relationships to be based on understanding, trust, and intimacy.

Be in the company of supportive and nurturing people who promote development and wellness.

4. Set Boundaries:

Set your priorities and values and establish them to others to keep healthy boundaries in your personal and working life.

Get used to saying no without feeling bad when needed and understanding that your time and energy are valuable commodities.

Rest and detach from technology and work obligations to renew and refuel your mental and emotional energy.

5. Practice Gratitude and Mindfulness:

Develop a daily gratitude routine by thinking about the things you are grateful for, large and small.Make mindfulness a part of your everyday life by focusing on what is happening right at the moment through activities like mindful breathing, body scans, and sensory awareness.

Observe and enjoy the beauty around you especially in the face of hard times and problems.

6. Seek Support and Professional Help When Needed:

Consult with close friends, family members, or even support groups for emotional help and direction during trying periods.

If you are having problems to deal with your wellbeing or you are having persistent symptoms of distress, consider seeking help from the professional that includes therapists, counselors, and coaches.

Keep in mind that seeking help is an indication of strength, not weakness, and that there are resources and individuals that are willing to help you on your quest toward healthy living.

These practical tips, coping mechanisms, and actionable steps, when adopted as a part of everyday life, enable the readers to empower themselves to better manage their plethora of well-being. Each person's road is distinct, thus, it is important to practice with different methods and techniques to determine the one that suits you best. Keep in mind that small, systematic steps to health can bring about big and permanent changes in the quality of life.

Summary of Key Takeaways

The author relates the story of how he found the link between welfare and financial success. His journey started with seeking success in the corporate world without end, and realizing material possessions and external validations only. Though, he found out that real richness does not come from that we own, but the way, we experience life and the effect we have on others.

To maintain well-being, he created limits, took care of himself, and fed his mind, body, and spirit. It dawned on him that true wealth should be not only in terms of monetary values but also through good health, emotional strength, and inner peace. He embarked on a path of personal development and improvement, concentrating on creating the fortune of wellness in all areas of his life.

The author realigned his priorities, revised success criteria, and adopted self-care measures including workouts, mindfulness eating, and adequate sleep. He also invested in personal development and lifelong learning, getting help from mentors and coaches.

With the comprehension of the concept of well-being, he introduced the principles of abundance and generosity into the everyday life, knowing that wealth is when you give it to others and make the world better.

The author's search for an equilibrium between material and mental health started with the knowledge that real wealth is not only about financial prosperity. He redirected his attention from such external indicators of salary raises or material things to comprehensive growth and satisfaction of an individual. Exercising was placed at the top of the list as it helped in the improvement of physical health and was considered to be the most influential on mental and emotional state.

Mindfulness practice and meditation was also an important part of self-care, as it allowed him to live in the here and now and develop an awareness. Participation in a mindfulness and self-discovery themed weekend retreat reconfirmed his dedication to the precedence of emotional and mental health.

With his self-care and personal growth on his priority plan, he was noticing the positive shifts in all areas of his life, more resilient, more connected, and thus more fulfilled. He came to the comprehension that success is a process of growth and self-awareness, not only an outside recognition.

Although there were disappointments and obstacles, the author understood that growth many times developed through the setbacks. Reaffirming the experience, and with the knowledge to do better, he learnt, that riches are not in the money one has, or the success of his career, but in the quality of his relationships, the depth of his experience and in the actions, he takes to keep his values in check.

The author is dedicated to leading a life of well-being, happiness, and with purpose. He cherishes self-care, personal development, and love. A great change in his happiness has been observed by him. Now he focuses more on the wealth of well-being, the quality of his experiences, and the depth of his relationships. We should practice self-care, emotional intelligence and stress management. We ought to also build upon resilience, foster close relationships, and set limits.

Participating in thanksgiving and awareness is significant as well. Strong support system from a community and professionals where necessary can assist to negotiate and maintain wellness. It is important to allocate time for one's hobby, exercise, meditation, journaling, regular sleep, and mindful eating.

Emotion monitoring can help uncover the underlying thoughts and beliefs and develop emotional intelligence. Mindfulness meditation, yoga or tai chi help in management of stress. Limiting and delegating responsibilities is creating an atmosphere of care. To build resilience, failures should be considered to be learning and growth opportunities.

CHAPTER SIX

FOSTERING MEANINGFUL CONNECTIONS

THE IMPACT OF POSITIVE RELATIONSHIPS ON MINDSET

I BELONGED TO THAT type of people who believed that the success was all about coming up in career and realizing the outside goals. However, in the course of my life, I have understood that real satisfaction is in the relationships one makes in the process.

Therefore, what have I ever done to create any meaningful relationships in my life? Though it was not always smooth sailing, it was surely worth the effort. Allow me to tell you some of the things I have learnt.

To begin with, I had to change my thinking. I stopped thinking of relationships as transactional or shallows, but as opportunities for real interactiveness and mutual development. I was aware to bring authenticity, vulnerability, and empathy to interactions – virtues necessary for the formation of genuine relationships.

Active listening is a major component in helping to create deep relationships. Rather than merely waiting for my opportunity to talk, I began to really hear what people were saying- their hopes, dreams, fears, and aspirations. I learned that when I truly listened and was in the moment, I could create deeper connections and stronger relationships.

Another critical element of creating valuable relationships is readiness to be represented as a whole personality, with defects and everything. I think that the vulnerability is not a vice but a virtue, and by opening up and being honest about my own fears and insecurities I was able to create a refuge for others to do the same.

Certainly, creating real connections also means spending time to sustain and develop those relations. This implies that one has to make contact frequently, enquire about the state of others and be genuinely interested in the life of others. It is about being with others when they require support, rejoicing in their victories, and being a listening ear in hardships.

Of the many things I have learned about fostering meaningful connections, however, is that it is not only the number of relationships but the quality. Rather than burning out trying to keep track of many acquaintances, I concentrated on growing several real friendships. I realized that such profound relationships brought me much more satisfaction and happiness than that which a shallow connection could produce.

Besides building relationships, I also tried to focus on my family at a familial level. I allocated specific time to my loved ones, maybe a family dinner every week or a family outing once a month. When I gave preferential status to quality time with my family, I found that our relationships became stronger and we enjoyed many memorable moments together.

Another critical factor of creating significant bonds is to be able to forgive and leave behind the past hurts. Grudges and resentment only create poison in our relationships and stop us from progression. I came to understand the significance of forgiveness- not only because of the other person but also for my inner peace.

Surely, creating real bonds is not a matter of what we do for others but also of who we are for ourselves. I came to the conclusion that self-love is not being selfish; rather, it is necessary to sustain healthy relationships with other people. And so, I went on to allocate time to activities that fed my soul – it could have been a good book, a serene walk in the nature, or even a hot bath to unwind after a long day.

I also discovered the necessity of setting the limits in relationships when to say no and when to put my own needs and health on the first place. Now, I found out that it is alright to take a break and get my strength back when I'm too challenged, and that this way I am only improving myself as a loyal friend, a loving partner, and a faithful family member.

Creating and keeping genuine relationships.

In a modern society that is saturated with superficial communication and digital noise, the creation of authentic relationships has become more significant. Therefore, how did I create and sustain real connections in my life?

To start with, authenticity matters. Early on I learnt that trying to be the person other people want me to be, brings superficial relationships without depth and meaning. Hence, I chose deliberately to be who I am. I stopped putting on masks and began living my quirks, weaknesses, and imperfections. And you know what? It was incredibly liberating.

Listening is one of the things that I have learnt with regard to developing genuine connections that it is not only about what you say but also about how you listen. I was always the good listener but I came to realize that in reality hearing a person – understanding what they hope for, what they are afraid of, what their dreams are and what their struggles are – is the basis of the real relationship. So, I have developed a habit of little steps – to put away my phone, to look into their eyes, and to give the person who speaks my full attention. And believe me, this changed everything.

Another significant part of creating genuine bonds is being vulnerable. I once considered that being vulnerable was a limitation, but now I feel that it's a power. Through letting out and revealing my fears, insecurities, and challenges to people, which also helped me bond with people at a deeper level. It's funny that being vulnerable can build an instant connection with someone – it's almost like saying "I trust you enough to show you the real me".

Certainly, building real connections also needs the effort rather than just creating them. Consistent presence is what it is all about, being available on a regular basis to offer support to people, and trying to stay connected despite busy schedules. What I found is that little gestures, such as sending a text just to see how another person is or arranging regular catch-ups really help in keeping the meaningful connection between people.

One of the things I've come to realize in building real relationships is that it's not about the quantity, - it's the quality. I refrained from being a friend to all, but concentrated on creating a handful of real good relationships. I put all my time and efforts in building those relationships and they have been repaid in ways that I could never have imagined. Deep, substantial relationships have given me more happiness and satisfaction than any shallow situations ever could.

One more critical factor of developing real connections is the ability to be accessible to others, even when it is not convenient. I've come to realize that a real friend is the one who is there for someone in his happy as well as in the difficult times – celebrating his victories, comforting him in the crises, and providing a shoulder to cry on when it's needed. It is all about giving a certain consistent and trustworthy presence in people's lives, even if it is not always an easy thing to do.

Naturally, authentic connections are also about being able to forgive and free oneself from past resentment. Allowing to us dwell on grudges and resentments only poisons our relationships and prevents us from moving forward. Forgiveness is something I have learned to be very important but not only for the other person but for my peace of mind as well. It's letting go the burden of the past and permitting ourselves to go on with an open heart and mind.

Reflecting on my adventure of creating worthwhile connections, I realize how fortunate I am to have many people in my life- the friends who have been a constant support, the family who has been by my side always and the leadership that has directed me through the path. My life has been enhanced by them in ways that I could never have contemplated and I will always be grateful for the love, strength, and support that they have given me.

So, if you're looking to foster more meaningful connections in your own life, my advice to you is this: be real, be sensitive, and be ready to work on these relationships in the long run. It can be challenging at times, but I am telling you: you will be glad that you did.

In the modern world of today, one can easily be carried away by the rat race of the daily activities. Most of the time, we end up handling a lot of tasks, from job and family, to social responsibilities and individual interests. Amidst it all, one of the most significant parts of our lives gets easily forgotten – our relationships.

Creation of bonds is crucial for our general health and mental well-being. It has been revealed that good social connections have influence on our mind leading to more happiness, resilience, and life satisfaction. However, the process of establishing and keeping real connection is not that simple, it needs energy, weak point, and readiness to be yourself. So, what is the way of living in rich relationships?

Here are some practical tips and actionable steps to get started:

Be Yourself: True connection is the base of meaningful relationships. Rather than trying to please others or fit into a social mold, just be who you are, peculiarities and all. Authentic people attract other authentic people who love them for who they are.

Practice Active Listening: The true listening to others is the base of establishing the genuine contacts. Rather than sitting and waiting for your chance to talk, try to listen actively – keep eye contact, nod to show that you agree, and ask a lot of follow-up questions to show that you are involved and interested in what the other person has to say.

Be Vulnerable: Vulnerability is not lack of strength; it is a strength. The fact of opening to and showing your fears, insecurities, and sufferings to others can make a strong bond and a trust between you. Be open to reveal who you really are and let others do the same.

Show Empathy: Empathy is the skill to perceive and partake in the feelings of others. Showing empathy to others tells people that you have consideration for their welfare and you are ready to offer support both in good and in bad. Cultivate empathy through an effort to understand the other person's point of view and by offering validation and support.

Prioritize Quality Over Quantity: A large network of acquaintances does not mean authentic connections but rather few, meaningful relationships. Spend of your time and efforts on developing those connections, and emphasize quality rather than quantity.

Be Consistent: Authentic relationships are built through having the patience and intention to know someone. Try your best to communicate with your friends and relatives on a regular basis irrespective of whether it's through phone calls, SMS or meetings. Be there for people regularly, even when it is not convenient.

Practice Forgiveness: Carrying grudges or resentment only destroys the relationships and the process to move on. Forgive by releasing the past hurts and live only in the present. You see, forgiveness does not mean that we condone or excuse the actions of the other person; it is about letting go of the negative energy and moving on with an open heart.

Set Boundaries: Boundaries should be set in order to have a balanced relationship. State your needs and priorities and assertively communicate them to others. Practice the art of no when needed and focus on your own health.

The development and nurture of real connections tend to greatly influence the nature of our mind set and general well-being. We are more supported, accepted, and appreciated when we have sturdy social support systems. We feel a sense of belonging and relatedness that provides us with the ability to move through life's adversities with resilience and dignity.

In fact, as those relationships become healthier, they also lift our spirits and add to the richness of life. We are one, as we rejoice each other, enjoy our time together and reminisce our past events. This is the thing that gives us a sense of worth and of belonging. Through the actual relationships we feel happy, accomplished and friendships touching—these things are not similar to monies and the other things buying.

To begin with, promote a true friendship by interfacing in a genuine manner, giving your full attention, and being honest with your understanding and acceptance. While many people aim at racking a big number of connections, it is time to consider linking with few high-quality individuals that make the life happy and fruitful. Finally, with other people, not how many relationships we have that sometime matters the most.

The cultivation of gratitude and motivation is the key to maintaining relationships. Along the way, communication, and timely feedback must be the guiding force. Given the choice between my childhood friends or the thousands of people I was exposed to in college, I would choose my close relationships every time.

In the modern era, people feel completely isolated when they are neglecting the significant bonds. Notice yourself the difference, when you talk to other people who are genuinely interested while applying the activities of listening. At the heart of any relationship, there is often a moment of vulnerability that bonds people together and leads to trust. As boundaries do for the fulfilment of our own needs, empathy and leniency, in turn, make a real bond.

We need to put genuine connections with others ahead of everything which makes our life fulfilling and this in turn affects our well-being with positive ways. Nothing easily compares to the thrill, comfort, and, unconditional love that one can get from someone they love. Having real people in the society who treat us genuinely in life is the actual thing that matters.

Summary of Key Take Aways

In relation to this, the author informs about the importance of having meaningful relationship in life for he says that success is not found in obtaining professional goals, but in the relations that one finds. They stress also on true 'self', honesty and understanding while speaking, active listening and desire to be looked at as a whole person. They also lay down the importance of giving time for maintaining and developing relations, continuous communication with people and real interest in the life of others.

The focus of the author is not so much on the number of relationships but on the quality of the relationships. He underscores the necessity to make living friends, to take care of the family, and to forgive. He also stresses upon self-love, and boundary in a relationship and allow to have self-care activities and timeout anytime.

Finally, the author reiterates that building deep relationships, substance over style, and self-love and self-care are the primary takeaways.

In a contemporary world, the essentiality of forming and keeping real connections becomes greater. Simple acts like ban of phone use, gaze into their eyes and be all ears can do magic. The vulnerability as well, can also be a very powerful force in establishing real connections. The presence should be constant, as being accessible to support and communicate anytime is important even in a busy schedule.

On reflection of the process of developing close relationships, the writer comes to realize the importance of having a friend, family members, and a supportive leader in his life. The long-term way is to build real, compassionate, and supportive relationships.

Relationships are an important part of our lives that are overlooked in the dynamic world of today yet they are vital to our total well-being and mental stability. Friend support leads to happiness, resistance, and life satisfaction. The virtues that should be developed to live in a fulfilling relationship include genuine behavior, good listening skills, vulnerability, understanding, value instead of quantity, consistency, forgiveness, and limits.

Real relationships are based on patience, intention, and communication and need to be about what a person desires and what he or she treasures. Forgiveness means going to the future with an open heart. Balance in relationships is based on boundaries, responsibility of your own needs and desires of others.

The formation and development of the proper relationships have a significant effect on the psyche and the health in general. They do provide us with strength, understanding and honor so that we can face the trials of life with fortitude and grace. Positive relationships bring us happiness and make our life colorful. Real relationships, understanding, all ears and genuinely grateful with tolerance and respect are some of the basics of being together.

Appreciation, inspiration, interaction and appropriate response are the components of relationship retention. The neglect of important connections makes people lonely today. The genuine characters, good listening, empathy, and sympathy, enable us to have real relations that brighten our life and enrich our good.

CHAPTER SEVEN

FINANCIAL MINDSET MASTERY

UNDERSTANDING THE PSYCHOLOGY OF WEALTH CREATION

PEOPLE WHO ARE TRYING to get rich usually don't pay attention to mental seize, but it's an important part of getting money for good. Since I've been living through the ups and downs of personal finance for the past few years, I know how important it is to have the right attitude on your financial journey. From now on, let's look more closely at the psychology of wealth, using real-life cases to help us understand what makes a person wealthy.

Management of the mental dimension of wealth generation

The ides and attitudes we have on money, mold our financial reality. Whether there is scarcity in our minds or abundance, the decisions we make and the actions that we take, are influencers of high degree. Reflecting and becoming aware is the step to knowing ourselves as well as the factors that limit our financial achievements.

Overcoming Limiting Beliefs

People often have restrictive and self-generated beliefs which they got directly from the childhood or from society's conditioning. We can, however, directly help ourselves to contribute to wealth creation by shifting these beliefs from a fixed to a growth mindset.

Illustrating Mindset Changes Case Studies in Wealth Generation

The Journey of Mark Cuban showing a mindset shift leading to wealth creation:

Background: Mark Cuban is an investment titan, successful businessman and CEO of Dallas Mavericks, an NBA team. While on the one hand he risked the conventional way of being successful, and nonetheless, he finally managed to achieve his goal. Jumping From a middle class family, born in Pittsburgh, Pennsylvania, Cuban showed signs of becoming an entrepreneur from his childhood.

Early Entrepreneurial Ventures: His very first time experience business activities boosted his energy and he later developed a keen interest in business. When the boy becomes 12 years old, he starts selling trash bags to make money to pay for his shoes of his favourite sport. He understood very early, that the beekeeping business provided little free time in addition to other overnight gainful activities that he indulged in, he got to know the value of hard work, perseverance, and frugality.

Mindset Shift: Despite all his excitement of entrepreneurship, Cuban first conformed to the mainstream and eventually started to pursue the traditional career path. He had graduated from Indiana University with the business administration degree and had some various jobs in technology prior to founding this company. Not until a big mistake in his plan gave him his "eureka!" moment, did he completely rethink his goals and turn his attention to making money.

The Dot-Com Boom: In the late 1990s when the dot-com era was in vogue, Cuban teamed with other venture capitalists to form Broadcast.com online radio company. Overcoming their scepticism and the resistance of naysayers was not easy for Cuban but he was unwavering in his resolve thus he continued to work on building a business.

Mindset Shift Moment: When Cuban offered to sell Broadcast.com to Yahoo! for a record-breaking amount of money in 1999, just before the dot-com bubble burst, the turning point came. The price was about $5.7 billion. Many people believe that Cuban made a mistake by selling so fast, yet he cashed in even though the future looked promising.

Post-Sale Success: Rather than taking it easy, Cuban turned the Broadcast.com sale proceeds into investments to venture further and grow his business realm. He worked in a variety of industries, including technology, sports branding, media, and entertainment, demonstrating the guts to take any risk in order to diversify his portfolio.

Lessons Learned: Cuban learned a key lesson: he could never control how long and easily he could accumulate riches until he was more aware of timing, resilience, and adaptation aspects. He understood that doing these things would help him to stay on top and that to succeed would require the persistence of innovation and of never allowing oneself to be satisfied.

Current Status: As of today, Mark Cuban is among one of the wealthiest humans on the planet, with a net worth above $6.2 billion as of 2023. He goes ahead with the startup investments, someone that views the world with fresh eyes, knowledge-sharing, and champions financial literacy, that gives others an opportunity to learn and try.

The real-life example of Mark Cuban successfully making a shift in his mindset, which resulted in the creation of wealth becomes compelling. Cuban earned the label of "success" by doing what others were not about to – daring to be different. He calculated the risks keenly, and he never gave up even when things got rough. He was transformed from a middle-class boy with big visions into a billionaire, entrepreneur, and philanthropist.

The journey of Cuban indicates that one's financial destiny is mainly the result of one's mindset, which is as powerful as theory of relativity and can always be successfully applied for a desirable result when the right attitude and determination are present.

In this section of how to create wealth, a real-life example of Mark Cuban displays the capabilities of the mindset to open the wealth creation potentials. Putting oneself in a mindset of abundance, resiliency, and risk-taking which is strategic will help a person to thrive even through hardships and eventually end up being very wealthy.

A Positive Money Mindset Congruence: cultivating gratitude and abundance mentality. Thanks is the most effective trigger-cause for prosperity. By doing this, we become aware of what we have and how much we appreciate it, this also helps us to realize that people who definitely know what they want and maintain their focus on abundance rather to scarcity, will definitely become those who are successful and prosperous.

Setting Clear Financial Goals

To be financially successful is to know when and where your goal is.

We make a detailed roadmap by setting clearly defined, measurable, reachable, relative and time bound (SMART) goals which guides our financial path and keeps us on track to accomplish them.

Making Increased Resilience in Adapting to the Financial Difficulties

There are economic problems that everyone has to deal with, and how we respond to them decides how things turn out in the end. Through building resilience and interpreting challenges as a chance to experience growth, we'll be able aim for a greater triumph and go on our financial freedom path.

Utilizing Visualization and Positive Statements Techniques for an Accelerated Mindset Transformation Techniques of Visualizing Financial curative Methods

Visualization – is a great device for seeing our desires and bringing them into being. When we picture our end goal in a clear and detailed way as if it has already happened, our conscious and unconscious minds will work together gaining momentum and bringing our goals to reality. Formulating Affirmations which help the individual to believe in her/himself within the framework of monetary matters.

Affirmations for self – these are the positive words that we repeat to ourselves to plant the idea in our mind about the things that empower us. By writing encouraging words or memories that help us remember why we are working toward our financial goals, we can access and change our deepest selves in order to be successful.

Here lets take a look at some real-life examples of individuals who used visualization and affirmations to achieve their financial goals:

1. Oprah Winfrey

Background: Oprah Winfrey, a media tycoon, and philanthropist is well known for her epic rise from poverty to a billionaire. All through her career, Oprah has utilized visualization and affirmations as her primary aids.

Visualization Practice: While she was in her younger years as a struggling TV host, Oprah used to picturize her trance to attain her goals in very clear details. She would visualize herself as a renowned talk show host who successfully interviewed celebrities and had fans all over the world. Affirmations for Success: Affirmations were also used by Oprah to strengthen her trust in herself and her powers. Daily, she would echo affirmative statements such as "I am worthy of success," "I attract abundance into my life," and "I am capable of achieving my dreams" both through her thoughts and by speaking them out.

Achievement of Financial Goals: Oprah visualized and affirmed consistently, and finally, she manifested her vision of success. Her talk show, "The Oprah Winfrey Show," became one of the highest rating television programs ever, making her a household name and a wealthy woman. She followed with a multimedia empire that included a television network, magazine, and production company, becoming an unprecedented financial success.

Legacy of Empowerment: Today, Oprah is a living symbol of empowerment and believing in oneself to millions of people all over the world. She inspires others to utilize the power of visualization and affirmations to realize their goals and live the lives they want.

2. Jim Carrey

Background: Another example of a person who practiced visualization and affirmations to reach his financial targets is Jim Carrey, a loved actor and comedian. Carrey was an impoverished and insecure nobody, before he became a Hollywood icon.

Vision Board Manifestation: Carrey is famously known as an actor who during his early struggling days wrote himself a $10 million cheque for "acting services rendered" and dated it on Thanksgiving 1995. He kept this cheque with him in his wallet and saw himself receiving money from his acting performances.

Daily Affirmations: However, in addition to the symbolic check, Carrey also had a routine of daily affirmations which he used to keep his thinking positive about his acting skills and his prospective future in the entertainment industry. He would confirm statements like "I am a famous actor," "I am creative and I deserve recognition," and "I attract profitable acting roles into my life."

Financial Success: The career of Carrey became a big success and he became known as a great comedic actor with many hit movies, such as "Ace Ventura: Pet Detective," "The Mask," and "Dumb and Dumber." Carrey got a check for $10 million for his part in the movie "Dumb and Dumber" just before Thanksgiving 1994. It was the same amount he had put on the check.

Lesson in Manifestation: The Carrey case is an excellent illustration of the law of attraction in practice. With the help of visualization, affirmations, and strong faith in his goals, he realized his monetary target and reached an unmatched success in the entertainment world.Oprah Winfrey and Jim Carrey are the two concrete real-life cases indicating how visualization and affirmations can help in achieving the financial objectives. Both of them applied the principles of law of attraction and by never losing faith in their dreams, they manifested phenomenal success and abundance in their lives.

Adopting a Growth Mindset Towards Financial Knowledge through Perpetual Learning and Self-Improvement.Lifelong learning is the key to being current and competitive in today's fast-moving economy. Through investing in our financial education and acquiring new skills, we put ourselves in the best position for a long term success in the market place.

Search for Financial Learning and Skill Building Opportunities

Through books, courses or mentorship we have many paths to broaden our financial understanding and skill. We empower ourselves to make educated financial decisions by being proactive in our search for learning opportunities and take advantage of profitable opportunities.

Success Stories of People who Changed their Financial Lives Through Education

Lets for a moment take a look at some real-life examples of individuals who transformed their financial lives through education:

1. Warren Buffett

Background: Warren Buffett, also known as the "Oracle of Omaha," is among the most prosperous investors in the world. Although he spent his childhood in a humble house in Omaha, Nebraska, Buffett's thirst for education and commitment to learning lit the way to his financial prosperity.

Investment Education: Buffett developed an interest in business at a very young age. His consumption of books on finance and economics continued as he was interested in the philosophy behind a successful investing. Buffett attributes his insatiable desire for knowledge as the main factor that enables him to spot potential lucrative investment avenues and maneuver the intricacies of the stock market.

Mentorship and Learning from Others: Moreover, aside from self-taught learning, Buffet also looked for gurus and professionals in the field of investment. One of Buffett's popular stories is that he was a student of Benjamin Graham, an iconic investor and author of "The Intelligent Investor" and a primary influence on Buffett's investing philosophy. Under the tutelage of Graham, Buffett mastered his analytical thinking and adopted a value investing approach that would become his investing strategy for years to come.

Application of Knowledge: Equipped with a sound understanding of investment principles, Buffett started to put his knowledge into practice. He became a stock investor from a young age and soon accumulated well-diversified portfolio of top-notch quality companies having competitive advantages and prospects of a long term growth.

Financial Success: With the passage of time, disciplined investing and lifelong learning became the drivers of Buffett's financial prosperity. His company, Berkshire Hathaway, became one of the most well-known and powerful conglomerates in the world, delivering great profits to its shareholders and significantly contributing to the popularity of Buffett as an investment deity.

2. Sara Blakely

Background: Sara Blakely, the creator of Spanx, is a self-made billionaire and a businesswoman that has found success among women of her era. The story of Blakely's attainment of success started from a modest background in Clearwater, Florida where she had to work at various jobs to support herself through college.

Entrepreneurial Education: Having no business or fashion schooling, Blakely knew the value of education in realizing her entrepreneurial dreams. She went in books, seminars, and online courses on entrepreneurship, marketing, and product development with the intention to know everything about how to build a thriving business.

Creative Problem-Solving: The education of Blakely was not limited to traditional ways as she adopted the approach of creative problem-solving and innovation. In her attempts to develop ideal undergarment she tried different materials and designs, drawing motivation from her own disappointments and consumer experiences.

Persistence and Resilience: Blakely experienced many setbacks and rejections but her dedication and the drive for learning never diminished. It was the way she used to see every challenge as a chance to make a better person of herself, to fix her approach and not to give up.

Business Success: Blakely's dedication to education paired with her entrepreneurial spirit saw her through when she came up with Spanx, a revolutionary line of shapewear, that she launched in 2000. Initially, Blakely's idea of an innovative product was met with scepticism from retailers and investors, but her clever marketing tactics and public relations propelled Spanx into unparalleled success, and Blakely became the youngest self-made female billionaire in history.

Continued Learning and Growth: Blakely, despite having reached remarkable success with Spanx, is dedicated to always learning and growing personally. She's very proactive in seeking the opportunities to learn and grow, understanding the fact that education is the key to being adaptive and competitive in today's fast changing business environment.

The live stories of Warren Buffett and Sara Blakely are evidence of how education can significantly influence financial success. By their commitment to study, use of knowledge, and unrelenting determination, They attained exceptional success and set an example for many others to follow their footsteps in pursuit of financial independence and prosperity.

Fear and managing fears in taking calculated risks and identifying and dealing with fear of failure and loss

Fear is of course the natural reaction to an uncertainty; however, it can also make us inactive and inhibit us from taking needed risks for the sake of development. When we approve our fears and convert them to learning and growing opportunities, we are able to defeat inertia and take action towards our financial objectives.

Risk Management Strategies in the Course of Financial Growth

Risk is always a fact of any financial activity, but with cautious planning it can be managed and controlled. With a balanced attitude to risk-taking and long-run orientation, we can work our way through swings and achieve the maximum potential.

Here are some real-life examples of individuals who conquered fear and took bold financial risks:

1. Elon Musk

Background: Elon Musk, the visionary businessman responsible for such companies as SpaceX, Tesla, and Neuralink, is characterized by his readiness to take extreme risks while pursuing his colossal targets. Even though Musk has had to deal with an array of failures and obstacles along the way, his daring approach to innovation has led him to great success.

Venture into Space Exploration: Musk's one of the most extraordinary financial risks consisted of the establishment of SpaceX in 2002 which had the purpose of changing the space travel. When the space industry was ruled by the government bodies and large aerospace companies, Musk invested millions of dollars of his own into the development of the reusable rocket technology and space missions.

Overcoming Scepticism and Failure: Musk received criticism and scepticism from industry experts that did not believe in the practicality of his grandiose plans. Nevertheless, he was unperturbed and wagered his whole fortune on the success of SpaceX and kept pushing forward despite numerous rocket failures and the brink of bankruptcy.

Achieving Milestones: The perseverance of Musk bore fruit when SpaceX accomplished several historic milestones such as being the first privately-funded company to send a spacecraft into orbit and return reusable rockets successfully. These achievements not only made SpaceX one of the leading suppliers of space exploration but also confirmed Musk's vision of making space exploration more accessible and cheaper.

Revolutionizing the Automotive Industry: Beyond SpaceX, Musk made another daring investment by buying into Tesla, an electric car company, when the whole concept of electric vehicles was still niche and not profitable. Although he was received with scepticism by investors and industry insiders, Musk pressed his views that he could speed up the world's transition to sustainable transport.

Impact and Legacy: Today, SpaceX and Tesla are worth billions and Musk is seen as one of the most successful and innovative entrepreneurs of all times. His ability to remove fear, take courageous financial risks and challenge the norm has not only reshaped industries but has also left millions of people all over the globe encouraged to chase their own dreams of innovation and disruption.

2. J.K. Rowling

Background: Another example is J.K. Rowling, a bestselling author of the Harry Potter series, conquering fear and taking a brave move to invest all she had to her passion. Prior to her literary achievement Rowling also had to live with adversities and uncertainties in her private and professional life.

Persistence in the Face of Rejection: However, after finishing college, she lived through difficulties of making a living and faced many failures in her writing career. She was turned down by numerous publishing houses that did not want to have anything to do with her first novel, "Harry Potter and the Philosopher's Stone", but she eventually found a publisher at Bloomsbury Publishing.

Financial Risk: Although she was given an upfront payment of only £1,500 for the first book in the series, Rowling invested herself completely in writing Harry Potter books, taking a substantial financial leap of faith with this endeavor. She spent her time, energies and resources without a guarantee of success in realizing her world of magic.

Overcoming Doubt and Self-Imposed Limitations: Despite doubts and fear of failure, Rowling fought them every step she took in her writing path. She overcame her fears, tapping into her imagination and creativity and wrote a story which would touch countless readers in the whole world.

Global Phenomenon: The Harry Potter series, however, turned out to be a worldwide phenomenon, with the books selling over 500 million copies in all the languages and leading to a multibillion-dollar franchise of books, movies, merchandise, and theme parks. Rowling's adventurous spirit allowed her to triumph over fear, take daring financial risks and keep fighting in the face of adversities—turning her from a struggling writer to one of the richest and most famous writers of all time.

The cases of Elon Musk and J.K. Rowling are the living examples of how conquering fear and making bold risky financial decisions can change one's life. Both individuals overcame their fears, accepted the unknown, and pursued their callings with unyielding perseverance only to succeed in a big way and to leave a legacy of inspiration for others to dare greatly and go after their desires.

Community Support and The Influence of Social circles on Financial Mindset

Our social environments have a huge impact on our money attitudes and behaviors. Our financial growth and success are supported by the presence of people we consider as our friends who also hold the same values and dreams with us.

Networking with Peers

Look for communities—both online and off—that could offer you the ability to connect with people who share your financial story. You can do more when you share knowledge, resources, and support.

Lets now have a look at some real-life examples of individuals who leveraged the power of community support in achieving their financial goals:

1. Muhammad Yunus

Background: Muhammad Yunus, a Bangladeshi economist, and social entrepreneur, is famous for his innovative work in microfinance and poverty reduction. The efforts of Yunus through his revolutionary project, Grameen Bank (Rural Banks), helped the poor people, especially women, to come out of poverty by providing them the small loans and community support.

Microfinance and Community Lending: Yunus saw that the traditional banking systems were out of reach for the poor as they did not have collateral and a history of credit. In turn, he started Grameen Bank in 1983 which was known for giving microloans and aimed to uplift the standards of living of the low-income earners. What made Grameen Bank's model different was that it involved peer support and community lending groups called "Grameen groups."

Empowering Women Entrepreneurs: The community lending groups of Grameen Bank were mainly composed of women, who worked together to back up their fellow women entrepreneurs. The weekly meetings allowed group members to offer support, controversial, and accountability to each other, enhancing a feeling of unity and mutual empowerment.

Financial Independence and Social Impact: The revolution that was brought by Grameen Bank community lending was quite significant as it enabled millions of women to become independent financially and pull themselves out of poverty. Utilizing the might of community assistance, Yunus changed the lives of many people and families, eliminating the cycle of poverty and leaving room for opportunities for sustainable growth.

Global Recognition and Expansion: The innovative stance of Yunus towards microfinance garnered him acclaim including the 2006 Nobel Peace Prize. The successes of Grameen Bank created similar projects across the world, thus initiating the global movement of inclusive finance and community-based development.

2. Dave Ramsey

Background: Dave Ramsey, being a personal finance expert, a radio host, and a bestselling author, is famous for his sound advice on how to get out of debts, how to amass wealth, and how to achieve financial freedom. By means of his highly listened to radio show, "The Dave Ramsey Show" and his Financial Peace University program, Dave Ramsey has helped millions of people to take control of their money and succeed in reaching their financial objectives.

Community-Based Financial Education: The power of community support is one of the principles of Ramsey's financial education. In the classes of Financial Peace University, people join in small groups to learn about budgeting, saving, investing, and debt reduction that is facilitated by trained facilitators.

Accountability and Encouragement: The small group of Financial Peace University promotes accountability and support between the participants which allows them to share their financial problems, victories, and goals for each other. This support network allows the individuals to remain inspired, navigate hurdles, and follow the path to their financial objectives.

Transformational Impact: Many people have been transformed by Ramsey's Financial Peace University program. Using community support as their aid, the participants have paid off debt, created emergency funds, saved for retirement, and have become financially independent, all the while cheering each other.

Legacy of Empowerment: The focus on the community support of Ramsey in financial education is a legacy that lasts, urging people to join hands, support each other and control their financial destinies. By his teaching, Ramsey has emancipated people from all classes to come out of financial shackles, live meaningfully and pursue their dreams with boldness.

Thus, the real-life cases of Muhammad Yunus and Dave Ramsey show the efficacy of social backing in financial aims accomplishment. The unity of individuals, the act of sharing, and both support and responsibility can empower an individual to overcome challenges, generate wealth, and secure a better life for his family.

Gratitude and Generosity Practice And The Relationship Between Gratitude, Generosity and Wealth
Appreciation and giving are virtues but also the main forces of prosperity generation. In this cycle of abundance, we are grateful for our blessings and by giving back to others, we double our richness while enriching others.

How to integrate gratitude and giving into financial practices.

Charitable donations, some random acts of kindness, or mere appreciation of what we have are ways to practice gratitude and generosity in our daily lives. Making the practices an essential part of our financial mindset, we synchronize with the abundance and bring prosperity to us.

Here are some real-life examples of individuals who demonstrated the transformative effects of gratitude and generosity:

1. Bill Gates

Anecdote: Bill Gates, one of the co-founders of Microsoft and one of the richest people in the world, has been a philanthropist for many years. In his annual letter to the Bill & Melinda Gates Foundation, Gates often provides personal stories which elucidate the power of gratitude and generosity.

Example: One of the anecdotes that Gates shares is about a visit he made to a small village in Africa where the Gates Foundation was working to improve the access to clean water and sanitation. The villagers, although suffering extreme penury and hardship, received Gates with warm heart, expressing deep thanks for the aid of the foundation.

Impact: The villagers' fortitude, appreciation and generosity, even in adversity, touched Gates deeply. Their attitude of thankfulness was an encouragement for him to work even harder in the area of global health and development and to direct more funds to projects that would help the most [deprived] communities in the world.

Legacy: Gates through his philanthropy work has shown how gratitude and generosity can transform and create a positive prize in the world. His devotion to charity and love of the suffering encourages many other people to adopt this spirit of charity and compassion.

2. Oprah Winfrey

Anecdote: Moreso, Oprah Winfrey, media magnate, and philanthropist, has shared personal stories that define the impact of gratitude and sharing in the transformation of her life.

Example: In one story, Oprah tells us about hosting an episode of her talk show which was dedicated to giving back to the less privileged. Throughout the programme, Oprah helped the poor single mother with a new car, cleared her debt, and gave her the funds to follow her dreams.

Impact: The act of giving back not only provided happiness and comfort to the receiver but also changed Oprah's life. She felt appreciative that she could help in someone's life and acknowledged the miracle of charity in bringing about good.

Legacy: The legacy that Oprah's generosity and the fact that she took the opportunity to use her platform for the good left a spirit of kindness and charity. By virtue of her model, she has ignited the spirits of millions of people to return back to their communities and to cheer others up.

The real-life, concrete examples of Bill Gates and Oprah Winfrey illustrate the power of gratitude and generosity in inspiring improvement in an individual and in a community. Their acts of kindness and philanthropy have led others to a life of gratitude, generosity and compassion, so the world will never be the same due to this ripple effect.

The financial mind set is a crucial aspect of obtaining enduring wealth and abundance.

Through the awareness of wealth creation psychology, empowering beliefs and habits, we can set ourselves free and lead the lives we want. I encourage you to apply the ideas we've talked about here to your personal and professional finances, knowing that if you have the right mindset, anything is possible.

Strategies of Successful Financial Goal-Setting and Planning

1. Put Quantified Targets to Your Financial Goals

Defining your financial goals clearly is highly necessary before you can start planning. If it's a down payment for a house, paying off debt, or saving for retirement, be detailed about what you want to accomplish and set practical time frames for each goal.

2. Prioritize Your Goals

All financial goals are not the same. Some might be more critical or significant than others. Set your goals in priority, considering their significance and urgency, with emphasis on the ones, which will have the most influence on your financial well-being in both short and long run.

3. Divide your objectives in smaller milestones.

Big, long-term goals can be mind blowing. Split them into small achievable goals that you can pursue one at a time. Celebrate at intervals, as you progress and adapt the plan according to any change in the situation.

4. Develop a Realistic Budget

A budget is an essential instrument of financial planning. Keep a close tab on your income and expenditure to know where your money is going and also the areas where you can reduce or divert expenses to your goals. Utilize the budgeting apps or spreadsheets to make the process simpler and keep your records organized.

5. Automated Savings and Investments

Automate your contributions to make savings and investments a way of life. Automate transfers from your paycheck directly to your savings account or retirement fund in order to guarantee that you are always allocating money towards what you desire without having to do anything more at all.

According to a study published in the Harvard Business Review, people who wrote down their goals were 42% more likely to achieve them as compared to those who didn't. Writing your goals down helps in bringing clarity on your objectives and also increases your commitment toward achieving them.

Research in the field of behavioral economics has demonstrated the fact that positive framing of goals enhances motivation and persistence. Rather than concentrating on what you do not want (debt), create your goals in terms of what you wish to gain (unbending power) – this approach can move you to act and ignite the process.

Financial goal setting along with planning is the integral part of financial achievements. Clear definition of your goals, their prioritization, the distribution of big goals into smaller milestones, the creation of realistic budget, and the automation of saving and investment will guarantee you a secure and bright future. Case studies and research findings reveal the magic of setting goals in attaining financial goals. Remember, the secret is in continuous actions and keeping your mind on your long-term vision, aware that each step you take guides you towards what you want to achieve.

Be it for retirement funds, purchase of a house or starting of a business, strategic goal setting and planning can pave the way to a brighter financial future. Begin today by setting your goals, drafting a plan and taking steps towards fulfilling your dreams.

Summary of Key Takeaways

An excellent knowledge of wealth creation psychology is paramount for a long-term financial success. Our financial truth is created by the way we think and feel about the money and letting go of the limiting belief can help us, reach the highest point of wealth that we can achieve. The case studies such as Mark Cuban, who is a well-known investor and entrepreneur illustrate that wealth creation can occur as a result of the shift in perspective. Cuban grew up in a middle class home and began to demonstrate a nascent entrepreneurial spirit. He co-established Broadcast.com that was one of the biggest flops of the dot-com boom despite his traditional career path. He sold the business to Yahoo! in 1999. to make a $5.7 billion gain, showing his willingness to diversify his assets and bear calculated risks.

Cuban learned during his trip the importance of time, resilience, and flexibility in producing wealth. He learned that success is only for those who stay ahead, embrace change and refuse to settle for mediocrity. Currently, with over $6.2 billion, Cuban is considered one of the richest individuals in the world.

Believing in abundance and gratitude, setting financial goals, being strong when things don't go as planned, and using visualization and affirmations are all money practices. Mindset of wealth, resiliency, and calculated risk-taking allows people to deal with challenges easily and reach their maximum financial achievements.

Affirmations and visualization are powerful tools for magnetizing financial wealth. We can lay a base for our financial goals by working out the subconscious and conscious thoughts together. Notable personalities who have practiced visualization and affirmations include Jim Carrey, an actor-comedian, and media empire personality and philanthropist Oprah Winfrey.

Winfrey created a multimedia empire and achieved the financial goal by using the method of meditation and confirmations that played a significant role in the success of her television show. His daily affirmations and visualization of his acting prowess were also significant for Carrey's acting triumphs.

In the dynamic modern economic system, further education is mandatory to be competitive and pertinent. By searching for prospects for financial education and skill development like books, classes, or mentorship, people can be more able to make wise judgments and capitalizing on profitable opportunities.

Great investor Frank Buffett was influenced by renowned investor and author of "The Intelligent Investor," Benjamin Graham. Buffett was able to realize unique financial success because he had a methodical approach to investment and was a constant learner, which resulted in the company Berkshire Hathaway, now one of the largest and most successful companies in the world.

Affirmations and visualization are powerful ways of achieving financial success. Those who seek opportunities for skill development and adopt the mindset of a lifelong learner in the area of financial education can definately succeed in their financial lives.

Sara Blakely, who invented Spanx, is a rich woman businesswoman. She grew up in Florida with her family and had to work multiple jobs to put herself through college. Blakely adopted creativity and innovative approach to problem-solving and the role of education in realizing her entrepreneurial dreams.

Blakely's determination to prosper and her consistent commitment of the learning in adversity and rejection.

The launch of Spanx, Blakely's revolutionary shapewear brand in 2000, was enough to illustrate that her devotion to education and her entrepreneurial enthusiasm have brought her success. Blakely's innovative creation and clever marketing skills made Spanx an absolute blockbuster; this occurred even when investors and retails expressed a bit of reluctance. This made her one of the world's youngest self-made female billionaires.

Fear of failure and loss is a feeling of people who are full of suspense and anxiety, they need to recognize this feeling by fighting it and consider taking risks in pursuits of success. A middle stance on risk, attention to details in planning and diversification, and a focus on long-term plans are some risk management strategies.

Elon Musk, the bright businessman who is the mastermind behind SpaceX, Tesla, and Neuralink, is known for his risky financial adventures and clear vision. Having entered the space exploration and automotive industries with SpaceX and Tesla, respectively, Musk's aspiration to make space exploration more accessible to the public was confirmed and solidified his status as a space industry leader.

In present, the market caps of SpaceX and Tesla are billions of dollars and Musk's bravery in defying the odds, taking calculated risks, and dismantling old norms have changed several industries and inspired others to pursue their own dreams of innovation and disruption.

Elon Musk and J.K. Rowling who is the best-selling author of a Harry Potter series are examples of individuals who have achieved success in their hobbies by overcoming fear and by taking bold financial risks. Rowling rejected many offers from publishers before she signed the contract for the creation off of her first book "Harry Potter and the Philosopher's Stone." Although she was paid a £1,500 advance for the first book in the Harry Potter series, Rowling gave her all in creating the books. Taking this step she also made a huge financial danger.

These real-life cases of J.K. Rowling and Elon Musk illustrate that fear can be defeated and great financial risks can catalyse transformation. Each of them realized large success and did leave behind a powerful legacy which still inspires people to take risks and pursue their dreams by ignoring their fear, accepting the uncertainty, and doing what they love to do until the end.

The social networks play an important role in the financial behavior and perception of individuals. When we surround ourselves with people who have the same ideas and aims, we create a conducive environment for success and financial prosperity. Building relationships with those who value what you value can help you and these people both improve and flourish more.

The Bangladeshi economist and social entrepreneur, Muhammad Yunus is famous for his remarkable work in the field of microfinance and poverty reduction. Yunus gave possibilities for the poor, women in particular, to leave poverty offering to them small loans and community assistance by means of this novel Grameen Bank (Rural Bank) project.

Dave Ramsey, the radio host and personal finance guru has taught millions of people to manage their money through community-guided financial education.

The most significant aspects of wealth creation are appreciation and giving to others because they set up a prosperous circle which benefits us and all the others around us. Act of kindness, appreciation or charitable giving can be incorporated into our financial rituals to bring us closer to the flow of abundance and hence, more wealth. Appreciation and charity are qualities of this. Personalities like Oprah Winfrey and Bill Gate are good examples of the wonderful impact which giving and gratitude can have on people and communities.

Prosperity is dependent on the mastery of the financial mindset. By understanding the psychology of wealth creation and adopting empowered habits and attitudes, we will actualize our highest potential and create the life we want. We can attain our greatest potential and architect the life of our dreams by implementing the ideas presented here.

Financial stability and wealth are the products of goal setting and planning. That is, regardless of whether we set up a business, purchase a house, or prepare for retirement, our chances of success will be significantly improved if we have an understandable plan and feasible tactics.

Financial goal setting and achievement are key to success in any industry. The creator of Spanx, Sara Blakely, revolutionized the undergarment industry by creating form-fitting, comfortable shapewear choices for women. She measured key performance indicators such as sales revenue, market share, and customer satisfaction to track her growth. Blakely developed a comprehensive plan, which embraced involvement of the consumer, marketing, distribution, and product development. She reinvested in R&D to develop technologically advanced fabrics and designs that were in demand by the customer. To position Spanx as a dominant player in shapewear industry, relevant tactics including celebrity endorsements, targeted advertising campaigns, and various alliances with retailers were carried out.

Money-wise, define your goals, prioritize them, subdivide them, budget realistically and create systems of savings and investments. Studies reveal that when goals are written down they increase the probability of success by 42%. Positive goal-setting accomplishes motivation and consistency, leading to decision and achievement. These steps can alter your financial trajectory and also enable you to attain some long-term objectives.

CHAPTER EIGHT

CULTIVATING PROGRESS AND PERSONAL GROWTH

DEVELOPING A CONTINUOUS IMPROVEMENT PLAN.

THE PASSION OF MY professional path is continuous striving for the perfection and self-improvement. Realizing the value of continuous growth and development, I started to make a complete plan aimed at a sustainable improvement in all the dimensions of my life. The first process in the quest for improvement was to carry out a comprehensive self-evaluation. I evaluated my strengths, weaknesses and development areas, drawing on past events and input from peers and mentors. This reflection helped me to get focuses where I should direct my attempts and define concrete objectives to increase my productivity.

To take stock of my strengths, weaknesses, and areas for growth, I embarked on a comprehensive self-assessment process that involved several key steps:

Reflecting on Past Experiences:

I started by thinking about my previous experiences, both professionally and personally. I reflected on my accomplishments, obstacles I had conquered, and the knowledge I had gained throughout my journey. This self-assessment helped me to see what I was good at and where I had shown competence or mastery, and where I had failed or faced challenges.

Seeking Feedback from Colleagues and Mentors:

I realized the significance of getting an insight from others, therefore, I was constantly seeking opinions from my colleagues and mentors. I had open and straightforward discussions with people whose point of view I appreciated, asking them to share their ideas about my strengths or weaknesses. Their comments gave me outside views that were of great value and made me aware of my own blind spots.

Conducting Self-Assessment Exercises:

I, however, supplemented the feedback of other people with self-assessment exercises in order to understand my strengths and weaknesses even more thoroughly. I employed instruments including personality tests, skill inventories, and SWOT (Strengths, Weaknesses, Opportunities, Threats) analyses to methodically assess my competencies and weak points. Through these exercises I was able to recognize recurrences and tendencies in my behaviour and my performance that enabled me to locate areas in which I needed to work for development.

Setting SMART Goals: Building on the lessons learned by reflecting on my past experiences and through the feedback of others, I develop specific, measurable, achievable, relevant, and time-bound (SMART) goals for myself. These objectives were consistent with my general goals and covered the issues I was considering to improve. Whether it was improving a particular skill, fulfilling a developmental need, or embracing a new challenge, every goal was created to drive my personal and professional development.

Creating a Development Plan: Having defined my strengths, weaknesses and performance gaps, I created my personalized development journey i.e. plan, and actions to follow to reach my targets. This plan contained specific action steps, which were aimed at turning my strengths into advantages, overcoming my weaknesses, and utilizing the possibilities for development. I found tools like education courses, coaching, or mentoring relationships that would back up my efforts to improve and help me stay focused on my goals.

After my proactive actions to analyse my strengths, weaknesses and the areas to develop, I got precious views into my abilities and laid the bases for further personal and professional development. Self-reflection and the spirit of always looking to improve the self, have helped me in being successful and reaching my objectives.

Having defined my goals, I made a structured plan that reveals the concrete steps of actions and timeframes for their realization. I developed Stage 1 of each goal into small steps and formed deadlines and consequences to keep the progress consistently moving.

Having carried out a comprehensive self-assessment of my strengths, weaknesses and areas for improvement, I appreciated the daunting task of generating a systematic plan that would drive my efforts to pursuing my goals. To ensure success, I followed a systematic approach that involved the following key steps:

Defining Clear and Specific Goals:

I started by classifying my aims in definite and quantifiable ways. All goals were in line with my main aims and were in those areas that I saw as a chance to improve. No matter if it was a promotion of a particular skill, pursuing a next career level, or fulfilling a personal dream, I always set a clearly defined and achievable goal.

Breaking Down Goals into Smaller Tasks: Having set up my general goals, I divided them to the smaller attainable tasks or action steps. This method helped me to advance slowly but surely to my goals. I specified the actions or tasks that should have been done in order to reach every goal, making sure that they were specific, possible, and could be achieved within the given time frame.

Setting Milestones and Deadlines:

To maintain an accountable state and monitor my progress, I establish specific targets and due dates for each task or action step. These landmarks were checkpoints for me and they enabled me to control the progress and make corrections if necessary. I introduced deadlines and by doing so, I achieved an urgency that kept me focused and committed to the goals I had set for myself within the particular timeline.

Identifying Resources and Support:

I found the resources and support networks that would assist me to reach my goals efficiently. This came with the identification of training programs, workshops, courses, or mentorship that would take my skills and knowledge in the relevant areas to the next level. I also sought support from peers, mentors and/or coaches who could help me specifically in the areas of guidance, feedback and accountability as I worked toward my objectives.

Creating a Visual Plan or Timeline:

In order to see my progress and to keep myself motivated, I made a visual plan or timeline that shows the sequence of tasks, milestones, and deadlines. This could be in the shape of a Gantt chart, a project management tool, or a simple checklist, based on my liking and the complexity of my set objectives. Presentation of my plan made me remain orderly and concentrated on steps required to reach my goals.

Regular Review and Evaluation:

Eventually, I took a self-check and assessment in order to be able to know the progress and the results achieved in relation to the goals. I reserve some time on a weekly or monthly basis to evaluate what I have done and come up with a plan if there any obstacles. This ongoing process of reflection and assessment enabled me to remain adaptable and quick to respond to altering conditions while moving steadily toward my objectives.

By adhering to these stages and devising a detailed plan with action steps and milestones, I have successfully transformed my objectives into practical results. This methodology fostered understanding, responsibility, and enthusiasm that allowed me to achieve early and steady progress on my goals and to foster ongoing improvement in other areas of my life.

One of the pivots of my strategy was lifelong learning. I looked for ways to grow professionally, either through formal education, workshops, or self-learning. I kept on increasing my knowledge and skills which made me updated upon industry trends and best practices, thus, I was ready for success in a changing world.

Apart from paying attention to the development of professional skills, I also considered personal development and wellness in my continuous improvement plan. I incorporated healthy behaviours into my daily rituals which included routine exercising and other mindful practices and living a balanced lifestyle in order to increase my overall resilience.

While running my continuous improvement plan, I stayed flexible and ready for any feedback, recognising challenges as opportunities for growth, rather than stumbling blocks to success. I adopted a learning mindset understanding that failures were unavoidable but could teach a lot.Gradually, the positive results of my hard work started to appear. I experienced advancement in my productivity, efficiency and overall satisfaction in both my work and life. Through continual effort and sticking to my plan, I made significant headway concerning my goals, and continued to develop and grow in my personal and professional life.

Reflecting on the progress of my path, I feel satisfied with the plan I have developed for the never-ending improvement and the fact that it has a positive influence on my life. I am still dedicated to the search of perfection and look forward to what my path will bring to me next as I continue my growth and development journey.

Measuring and appreciating success : Establishing Measurement Metrics

In order to track progress efficiently, I defined concise measurement metrics that were consistent with each goal and milestone contained in the plan. The metrics were defined, measurable, and quantifiable, thereby, enabling me to objectively track my improvement over time. It did not matter if it was following up on the task completion, accomplishing particular performance targets, or meeting milestones in a certain period of time, having the set of metrics allowed to have a clear foundation to check progress.

Utilizing Tracking Tools and Systems:

I used different tracking technologies and systems to track in a systematic manner. These could be project management software, spreadsheets, or even just plain pen and paper if the nature of my objectives is of such simple structure. These instruments made it possible for me to keep a record of finished assignments, monitor milestones and visualize progress in the course of time. Keeping these tracking systems current allowed me to be organized and inspired, to see the road to my goal.

Setting Regular Check-In Points:

Apart from continuous monitoring, I set up regular check-in points to evaluate the process and identify any drifts from my plan. The check- in points could occur every week, every two weeks or monthly which depends on the timeline and urgency of the goals. In these check-ins, I assessed my performance against the set metrics, identified any obstacles or challenges, and made necessary changes to my plan to ensure that I stayed on course.

Reflecting on Achievements:

Rewarding successes was part and parcel of my progress-monitoring routine. I gave thought to and recognized the milestones I had surpassed on the journey. Such introspective reflection enabled me to value the achievements I had made, appreciate the effort I had exerted, and strengthen the determination to pursue my objectives. Be it a minor triumph or a major success, I rewarded each accomplishment as yet another step in my walk to personal and professional development.

Expressing Gratitude and Recognition: Besides cheering for my own accomplishments, I thanked those who have helped me in the process. This may entail co-workers, tutors, buddies or even family members who had given me direction, morale, or help along my way. Recognizing their contribution not only enhanced my support system but also developed a sense of fellowship and shared victory.

Rewarding Myself:

One of my self-care and motivation techniques was to occasionally treat myself upon reaching an important milestone or accomplishing a difficult goal. These treats could be diverse and could include doing one of my favorite things, having a nice meal or taking time to rest and relax. In recognizing my attempts and rewarding me, I strengthened positive behaviors and kept up the momentum for ongoing improvement.

Maintaining a Growth Mindset:

Though the monitoring and festive reports, I used an approach of learning mindset, seeing the failures as an opportunity for learning. If I met obstacles or failed to reach the target, I would regard these experiences as precious lessons and changed my methods correspondingly. I managed to keep my eye on long-term goals and cope with difficulties due to such resilience and adaptability.

Upon these methods being incorporated into my progress monitoring and celebration regimen, I was able to sustain drive towards my objectives and foster a feeling of success and pleasure throughout the process. Celebrating accomplishments had the role of strengthening the desired behavior and also reminded that I should constantly strive for excellence everywhere.

Embarking on the Journey of Holistic Prosperity: Words of Wise Ones

Today, in a very dynamic world, true prosperity goes beyond just wealth in material form. It is an integrative concept that covers physical energy, mental resistance, significant relationships, ongoing learning, and a purposeful social contribution. Now, let us investigate how some of the celebrities have embodied this holistic journey to success.

1. Oprah Winfrey: Developing Inner Unity

Oprah Winfrey is a prominent media personality and philanthropist who is the epitome of a holistic success seeker with her relentless commitment to the self-carer and self-seeker.Oprah has confronted many challenges in both her personal and professional life, but she has never lost her dedication to nurturing her physical.mental, and spiritual health.She shows her faith in holistic living through books, wellness products she endorses and spiritual teachings.By illuminating the unity of body, mind and spirit, Oprah inspires the people from the world to start their journeys of holistic success.

2. Elon Musk: Self-Care and the Pursuit of Success

Elon Musk, a visionary entrepreneur and inventor of revolutionary firms such as SpaceX and Tesla, serves as a living model of how to manage to align between self- care and ambition in the search of holistic well-being of oneself.Despite the fact that Musk must compromise himself for the sake of some big projects, he appreciates the importance of maintaining his physical and emotional health.He demonstrates that success is not only measured by external achievements but also on the person's inner welfare by incorporating mindfulness exercises, healthy eating, and exercising regularly into his busy routine. The Musk's example proves that the one should preserve the balance between ambition and self-care to ensure the complete prosperity.

3. Michelle Obama: Establishing Highly Significant Relationships

The former first lady of the United States, Michelle Obama, a great supporter of social issues, identifies the necessity of profound relations in the attainment of comprehensive success. Michelle has devoted her entire life to creating strong and worthy relationships with her family, friends, and communities. She emphasizes that creating powerful relationships should involve mutual understanding, compassion and support. Michelle shows how real human bonds promote overall welfare and another type of achievements on the road to holistic success through creating these relationships.

4. Richard Branson: Adopting Ongoing Enhancement

Richard Branson is a living icon of a modern entrepreneur and an explorer; he himself represents the human spirit that remains in search of ultimate wealth. During the years of successful entrepreneurship, Branson has been a man of changes, many interests, and lifelong learning. He tells people to get out of their comfort zones, embrace uncertainty, and use opportunities for career and personal growth. Branson demonstrates how willingness to change and seeking constant improvement bring joy and prosperity in all aspects of life through creation of creative and adaptive culture.

5. Malala Yousafzai: Service Development

Malala Yousafzai, an inspirational campaigner and Nobel laureate, is an embodiment of the transformative ability of social contribution to holistic prosperity. Malala remained committed to the struggle for girls' education and human rights even in adversity and danger. In her role, she uses her status to promote awareness of vital social concerns and promote global change. Malala serves as a case in point that contributing to the improvement of the society creates a sense of purpose, and along with it, basks in the glory of holistic prosperity given that she practices what she preaches and has a huge influence on the world.

6. Dalai Lama: The Development of Love and Inner Peace

The Dalai Lama is the religious leader of Tibetan Buddhism and a living model of mindfulness, compassion, and inner peace. Millions of people everywhere are awed by the Dalai Lama's composure and goodness in heart while living in banishment from his own country. His teachings of altruism, compassion, and meditation, stress the importance of developing inner peace and practicing kindness toward others as essential components of holistic prosperity.

7. Serena Williams: Balancing Self-Care and Success.

Serena Williams, a tennis player and a business person, demonstrates how to maintain the equilibrium between personal and professional achievements. In spite of the many accolades and achievements that Serena has bagged on the court, she ranks self-care and mental wellness at the top of the list. She talks openly about her struggle with body image, parenthood, and self-doubt offering a way to facilitate greater acceptance of mental health issues. Serena demonstrates that real abundance comprises health, beauty, and spirituality in addition to financial wealth through self-preservation and seeking support.

8. Nelson Mandela: Conciliation, Adaptability, and Forgiveness

Nelson Mandela, who was a celebrated anti-apartheid activist and former South African president, is an embodiment of forgiveness, resiliency, reconciliation and other values in the pursuit of holistic prosperity. Mandela emerged from the jail after 27 years having been imprisoned for his activism, forgiving and with an aspiration to build a more inclusive and equal society. Through his leadership, he made love and peace the cornerstones of a democratic South Africa. The legacy of Mandela is a powerful lesson that commitment to social justice, forgiveness and perseverance is what real success is all about.

9. Ellen DeGeneres: Happiness and Goodness to the World

The TV anchor's darling and a philanthropist, Ellen DeGeneres, embodies the notions that happiness and compassion are important components of the full human flourishing.Ellen offers a platform for good-will, laughter, and joy through her talk show on a daily basis. She takes advantage of the platform to promote philanthropic initiatives, preach inclusivity and tolerance, and participate in various social causes. By sacrificing a small part of prize Ellen shows how small actions can make a change on somebody's life and societies well-being.

10.Mahatma Gandhi: Truth, Simplicity, and Nonviolence.

Gandhi, the great leader of the Indian independence movement, is an archetype of the ideals of simplicity, truth, and non violence as means to holistic prosperity. Although Gandhi faced enormous challenges and pressures, he never relented in his pursuit of truth and nonviolent resistance. By his leadership he persuaded millions of people to practice simplicity, develop inner strength, and seek social justice. Gandhi's impact is still felt by individuals around the world who strive for both personal and collective prosperity based on the qualities of truth, love, and nonviolence.

Such bright instances reflect that holistic prosperity is a multidimensional concept, which includes sound physical condition, mental strength, the strong relationships, meaningful societal contribution, and spiritual satisfaction. Taking cues from individuals such as the Dalai Lama, Serena Williams, Nelson Mandela, Ellen DeGeneres, and Mahatma Gandhi, we could get many valuable ideas about how we can lead a life that is balanced, meaningful, and fulfilling in today's chaotic world.

Let's extract some practical tips from the examples of individuals who have attained holistic prosperity:

Prioritize Self-Care: Emulate Oprah Winfrey and take care of yourself by tending to your physical, mental, and spiritual health through activities such as exercise, healthy eating, meditation, and self-analysis.

Balance Ambition with Self-Care: Be Elon Musk and keep the harmony between being ambitious and taking good care of yourself. Be passionate about your goals but have time for rest, relaxation, and activities that refuel your energy.

Invest in Meaningful Relationships: Take a cue from Michelle Obama and focus on creating strong and significant relationships with family, friends, and communities. Spend time and effort on developing those relationships which makes happiness, comfort and satisfaction in life.

Embrace Lifelong Learning: Learn from Richard Branson and adopt an attitude of constant development and discovery. Learn opportunities, move out of the comfortable zone, and see change as a fourth revolution.

Contribute to Society: Learn from Malala Yousafzai and look for ways of serving the society. Employ your abilities, assets, and clout to lobby for social issues, to aid in charitable organizations, and to benefit your community and the world.

Cultivate Inner Peace: When following the teachings of the Dalai Lama, you should focus on methods that lead to inner peace, for instance, meditation, mindfulness, and compassion. Cultivate serenity and equanimity that allow you to find your way through the adversities of life in a graceful, resilient manner.

Balance Success with Self-Care: Borrow a leaf from Serena Williams' book—reach a balance between professional success, self-care, and mental health. Put your wellbeing ahead of everything, ask for help when you need it, and set boundaries to guard your physical and emotional health.

Practice Forgiveness and Resilience: Follow in Nelson Mandela's path of forgiveness, steadfastness, and conciliation. Forgive grudges, welcome adversity as a chance to develop, and pursue harmony and teamwork in your social and working relationships.

Spread Joy and Kindness: Be Ellen DeGeneres' disciple and take joy and kindness to every place you visit. Seek for ways to make someone's day, perform acts of goodness, and use the space you occupy to spread love and unity.

Embrace Simplicity and Truth: Get inspired from Mahatma Gandhi's principles of simplicity, truth and nonviolence. Eliminate the complicating aspects of your life in being surrounded by those that have been positive influences in your life and other things that really matter. Live genuinely with virtue and truth and make peace with conflict through dialogue and understanding.

With the help of these practical tips, you can create holistic prosperity and lead a well-balanced, purpose full and fulfilled life.

Summary of key Takeaways

The author started with self-assessment by reviewing his past experiences and feedbacks from colleagues and mentors. He afterwards carried out self-evaluation exercises through using instruments such as personality assessments, skills inventories and SWOT analyses to determine his competences and areas of development.

The author established SMART goals, which were in consonance with the general aims and addressed the areas for improvements. He came up with the individual development plan that contained the specific actions necessary to achieve these objectives. These actions included detailed plans on how to capitalize on the workout opportunities, steps to correct their weaknesses and ways of using and taking advantage of their strengths.

The author also created a detailed plan that outlined what needed to be done with milestones. He would break down each goal into small, achievable steps and implement deadlines and accountability measures for a constant progress. He recognized assets and tools like training programs, work-shops, courses, or mentorship opportunities that would enable him to attain his objectives efficiently.

To monitor his advances he made a visual plan or timeline that could be in the form of a Gantt chart, project management tool, or just a list. Periodic review and assessment helped him to be adaptable and alert to changes while keeping his momentum towards the target.

The systematic manner of self-evaluation, self-analysis, and a well-structured plan for continuous improvement has made the author successful in his life and goals attainment. Such approach ensures the transparency, the accountability, and the motivation and as a consequence, the man achieves a success in reaching his goals and improve all areas of his life.

The author's system of continuous improvement included a dedication to learning, professional development and personal growth. He looked for professional development opportunities by way of formal education, seminars, and self-teaching thus being up to date with concepts and best practices of the industry. He emphasized individual development and health, by integrating such habits as exercise and mindfulness. He was flexible and receptive to feedback, interpreting obstacles as a chance for improvement.

In time, he found these outcomes in production, efficiency, and overall contentment with his life and work. He persevered and stayed devoted to the project, thus, making considerable progress towards his targets.

In order to monitor the progress, he made concrete measurement metrics that were related to every milestone and target. To monitor advances, he utilized a bound of tracking systems and tools such as spreadsheets, project management software and even pen and paper methods. Check points were installed at a period to check on the system and identify any deviation from the original design.

A significant element in his keeping track of his progress was the celebration of victories, as this made him observe what he has already achieved and, in turn, restored his excitement for the oncoming way. He established his support network by showing gratitude and appreciation to those who helped him. We sometimes spoiled them when they accomplished crucial life events or hard tasks.

He persevered some challenges and stuck to his ultimate mission because he fostered a learning attitude. By integrating these strategies into his tracking and celebration regimen, he sustained his momentum toward his goals and at the same time established a feeling of achievement and happiness.

Holistic prosperity reflects relationships, intellectual strength, physical vigour, permanency, and social responsibility apart from money gains. These experiences were also shared by personalities including Oprah Winfrey, Elon Musk, Michelle Obama, Richard Branson, Malala Yousafzai, the Dalai Lama, Serena Williams, Nelson Mandela, Ellen DeGeneres, and Mahatma Gandhi.

Oprah Winfrey is focused mainly on development of the inner wholeness, which she advertises via various books, wellness products, and spiritual teaching. Elon Musk sees self-care in working out, healthy eating and even mindfulness techniques. The strategy that Michelle Obama employs in developing meaningful relationships is grounded on mutual support, understanding, and empathy. Richard Branson is a person of variety and promotes the lifestyle of lifelong achievement. Malala Yousafzai is an advocate for human rights and girls' education which is mostly done through action empowerment.

The live example of the Dalai Lama attracts and inspires millions of people all over the globe. Away from her numerous awards and the records which she sets on the court, Serena William has mastered the art of living in harmony between her personal needs and her achievements in the career. Forgiveness, resilience, and reconciliation are best illustrated by Nelson Mandela in total success. Ellen DeGeneres is a talk show host, a supporter of humanitarian organizations and an ambassador of kindness and joy. Mahatma Gandhi embodies the ideas of completeness of simplicity, honesty and nonviolence.

In doing so, we may get some practical counsel of how to live a complete, meaningful and successful life in today's world.

Proper self-care is a key to complete success. Other significant features comprise of making relationships, loving learning, helping others, keeping inner peace, and practicing self-care qualities such as resilience, forgiveness, joy, kindness, simplicity, and truth-telling. Individuals who have achieved complete success can be inspired by the following noteworthy figures: Malala Yousafzai, Serena Williams, Nelson Mandela, Ellen DeGeneres, Richard Branson, Oprah Winfrey, Elon Musk, Michelle Obama and Gandhi. Their life story help us live in harmony with a well-defined sense of purpose and contentment.

CHAPTER NINE

CONCLUSION

To sum up "The Positive Thinking Mindset," it should be mentioned that positive thinking influences your life in a number of good ways. As seen in the preceding chapters of the book how the material world of positive thinking can impact what happens in real life.

Positive thinking can lead to increased motivation, productivity, and overall happiness. By focusing on positive thoughts and beliefs, individuals can attract more opportunities and success into their lives. It is important to remember that cultivating a positive mindset takes practice and dedication, but the benefits are well worth the effort.

The positive thinking is completely transforming. Through a corrective lens of optimism or positive thinking, we allow this world into our comfort zone. This world is full of options and can provide us with happiness and a sense of meaning.

Starting right now, we recognize challenges as opportunities to advance, blocks as momentary objections, and failures as enriching educational experience. Such a turn of mind helps us to be stronger and to consider a challenge as a motor to our mental growth once we accept life's ups and downs.

In a nutshell, "The Positive Thinking Mindset" has concentrated on the power of positivity and its effects on the people. We not only benefit from an upbeat attitude, but we spread an encouraging atmosphere everywhere we go. Our optimism evolves into a contagious disease that stimulus others to adjust a similar stand and accordingly creates a wave of positiveness that rolls within our communities to the whole world at large.

In this case, the book not only shows the value of gratitude in life but acts as a tool that cultivates a positive mindset for every one. We learn to be thankful regularly. This way, our brains are retrained to highlight the richness in the life being lived, not the emptiness. The act of gratitude is such that it is much simpler than that but is also powerful that it is capable of changing the way we perceive things around us and consequently develops a profound feeling of fulfilment and contentment.

As a part of the "The Positive Thinking Mindset," visualization and affirmations were regarded as helpful in bringing of our desires into reality. We can jump-start the process by using visualization to already experience our outcomes and by telling ourselves, "Yes, I can!" which serves as a command for our subconscious mind.

This aspect isn't just about self discovery but will provide us assurance and positive outlook that can even lure more opportunities and resources that are suitable to our path.

In truth, "The Positive Thinking Mindset" is not just a book, but also a guide to having purpose and satisfaction laced with endless abundance in our lives. Honoring the values unveiled in the book and allowing ourselves to develop a healthy mindset polishes the life like a diamond. If we can own our own selves, we can also create the meaningful life. The Positive Thinking Mindset has thus ended. Therefore, let us take the wisdom imparted and venture on a trip of the endless prospect and wholistic effects of positive thinking.

Join Us in Shaping "The Positive Thinking Mindset" Together!

Invitation for Feedback

Dear Reader,

I welcome you all warmly, every one of you, the fellow pilgrims on our mission of exploring the art of mindfulness. It is my privilege to introduce and be a guide to you aboard "The Positive Thinking Mindset" course. I am more than excited and overwhelmed with much gratitude to share this memorable journey with you.

My initiative to empower those who have lost their identity involves me acknowledging the importance of your personal account, inputs, and understanding. Your journey to gaining self-esteem and mental fortitude, as well as mastering positivity, self-love, and owning challenges in whatever way you can, makes your route as distinctive as you are. The many viewpoints that comprise us simply add fuel to the fire and consequently increase our intellectual wealth.

Therefore, I expressively request your dwelling through the sharing of your opinion, impressions and stories with the publication "The mindset of a positive thinking person" as nothing is more valuable than your thoughts for the group of readers who thrill to be enlightened and enriched by everything positive.

I hope some of the ideas in this section can be something that can really change your perspective of being lost. Whether that be people who have found a particular a chapter particularly enlightening, when they discover new way to tackle hardships and biggest lights that have switched on in their brains when they are exposed to a new perspective about being lost. Your stories are empowered to create the engagement that may put the spark of hope and inspiration to other people who are probably are in a situation just the same as yours.

Be the seed that will help us cultivate a brighter future chapter wise, and will additionally develop a close-knit community centered on encouragement and personal development.

Here's how you can share your feedback:

Leave a Review: If the philosophy of positive thinking found in "The Positive Thinking Mindset" has proved helpful to you and guided you in your life, we appreciate that you take the time and leave a review on Amazon, Goodreads or any other platform where you acquire the book.

Join the Conversation: Contact me and join the rest of the readers and the participants of this movement on social media platforms with the hashtag #PositiveThinkingMindset to be part of this conversation. Gather around your favorite material and pass around quotes, inferences, and insights you have gathered from the book or simply share your experience of the book with others who are on a similar path to what you are.

Send me Your Stories: Please feel free to email the story/testimonial to connect @manjultewari.com for considerations or submission to various platforms. Can be highlighted on my website or social communication channels (of course, with your consent) as a method of encouragement for others to try.

This feedback is not your individual opinion suffice; rather, it is the beacon that will show the others the way. In summary, we are all avenues to wellbeing, overcome the negativity, and bring upon our people kindness and strength.

I hope that your time spent here has been nothing short of exceptional. Thank you for being an active participant in this extraordinary experience. Unity sears optimism in hearts. Positive change comes from each of us joining the efforts, and here science says: One positive thought at a time.

With gratitude and optimism,

[Manjul Tewari]

160

FULL BOOK SUMMARY

CHAPTER 1: POSITIVE THINKING Power Understanding

The story is about a man, who is waiting to catch a train, which will never come. This is when he encounters a man called Sam who imparts the philosophy that most events can be turned into the best opportunities. This shift of perspective leads to precise comprehension of the small things of life and positive attitude in mental health. Optimistic attitudes nurture gratitude, acknowledgment, self-improvement, therefore, healthy body and mind, immunity, and networking. It also leads to better cognitive performance, lower risk of cardio disorders, and professional achievements. Gratitude journaling, mindfulness meditation, positive affirmations, visualization exercises, challenging negative thoughts, self-compassion, setting achievable goals, engaging in positive hobbies, positive community contacts, and seeking support are some of the methods for a person to nurture a positive mindset. By and by, such practices can be customized to individual tastes and lifestyle and gradually incorporated into everyday life.

Chapter 2: Overcoming beliefs that limit.

Leonardo da Vinci, a Renaissance Italian polymath, had self-imposed limitations and challenges in his pursuits. The various interests including painting, engineering and anatomy made him regard his polymathic nature as a handicap. Yet, a mentor by the name Verrocchio helped him to realize his gifts and rid himself of self-doubt. Leonardo amalgamated his skills, combining his anatomical studies and engineering skills into his art. This tactic enabled him to rise above the restrictions of the day and produce some masterpieces such as Mona Lisa and The Last Supper. His legacy in this context is a source of light to those who are in a constant fight with their inner barriers and who question themselves. It is a clear example that being multi-facet can lead to innovative creation like no other.]

Throughout career, Thomas Edison, a prolific inventor, confronted many obstacles and limiting beliefs. He understood his particular style of learning and sought self-directed learning, taking failure to be evolution. Being attacked by the critics Edison nonetheless, continued his innovations, and in the end, he was appraised as the paradigm of inventor working on the most cutting-edge machines. He adjusted to changes, accepting the alternating system which turned out to be more convenient. His type of leadership was characterized by inspiration and guidance of a team, nurturing a setting in which various talents could prosper.

The breakthroughs of Edison, such as the electric light bulb and the phonograph, broke the established norms of the modern society, showing that the unconventional thinking could bring a radical change. The impact of his legacy is not measured by the plenty patents he held but also by the paradigm shift he brought to innovation and entrepreneurship.

New studies have investigated approaches to overcome limiting beliefs, through cognitive restructuring, a growth mindset, the use of neuroplasticity, gratitude and positive affirmations, as well as social support. These approaches make people rise above the limitations they had set for themselves and move towards their objective. However, the success of combating limiting beliefs is usually determined by individual factors, and personal strategies, which use several approaches depending on a person's individual circumstances, can produce the most effective solutions.

The process of recognizing and addressing self-limiting beliefs is an important part of personal development and reaching one's full potential. In order to do that, develop self-awareness, question your beliefs, seek feedback, identify triggers, change your negative thoughts into the positive ones, use affirmations, achieve realistic goals, practice mindfulness meditation, make positive visualization, think in a different way about catastrophic thinking, keep a thought journal, challenge comparisons, embrace continuous learning, and look for support from professionals.

To convert negative thoughts, develop gratitude practices, gain from failures, utilize positive self-talk, and counteract perfectionism. Concentrate on the bright side of your life and accept and value the blessings in your life. Turn setbacks into learning and growth opportunities treating them as part of a defining the path towards progress. Observe your internal monologue and substitute self-critical thoughts with beneficial and kind self-talk.

Keep in mind that reframe of negative thoughts is a continuous process and should be done persistently and with patience. Adding these methods into your everyday routine can develop a mentality, which allows you to achieve more, and fulfill your true potential. Reframing negative thoughts can be done by gratitude practice, learning from setbacks, constructive self-talk, and challenging perfectionism. Consistency and patience are the answers in incorporating these methods into your life on a daily basis, and in time you will find yourself practically prepared to maintain a more positive and resilient mind frame.

Chapter 3 : The Growth Mindset Mentality

The author's life has been revolutionized by progressive minded thinking. It is the belief that with the right mentality, everything is possible and that failures are opportunities for personal growth. This type of thought is developed through individual experiences and choices rather than something that is inherent.

The value placed on education and hard work by the author's grandfather's family set the course for his development of a growth mindset. Despite many of the failures, he chose to look at them as opportunities for growth. His determination to carry on his studying despite the lack of funds and objections from others gave him the confidence in the importance of education and hard work.

The story of the author's grandfather is evidence of the potential of faith, perseverance and lifelong learning. It inspired the writer that thinking and not surrounding factors determines the level of success. The author's grandfather has been a source of inspiration for him throughout his life, teaching him lessons of hard work, hope, and perpetual learning.

We do not have a growth mindset by nature but it is developed through the experiences and choices we make. Even the toughest obstacles can be overcome if we regard problems as opportunities, failure as part of success and have trust in our ability for growth and adjustment.

In conclusion, the growth mindset approach is a good example of the fact that everything is possible when one has the appropriate mindset. Resilient living and determined lifestyle is a way for people to overcome any challenge and successfully achieve their dreams.

The chapter covers a number of techniques of the problem solving and achieving long run success. It advises re-thinking challenges as opportunities for learning and growth, setting achievable goals, becoming resilient, practicing self-compassion exercises, receiving feedback, and focusing on reflection.

Progress can as well be controlled by dividing large targets into smaller achievable measures.

Resilience development is central to mental health results and situational adaptability. Good peer, mentors, family and friends support can be of much help during difficult times since they will offer both support and direction. To reinforce your attitude of resilience, you could rephrase negative thoughts into positive affirmations which you repeat over and over.

Self-compassion practice is associated with emotional resilience and lower levels of stress, anxiety, and depression. Self kindliness helps one rise up stronger in moments of failure or difficulty.

Feedback seeking is significantly related to career success and job performance. The usage of constructive criticism from a reliable coworker, mentor, or boss helps you find blind spots and points of growth.

In the long run, focus on personal care and self-improvement will help individuals to resolve challenges and gain success in the end. By adopting these tactics, people can develop a resilient mindset, improve their mental health, and achieve lasting success.

Reflect and learn: Regular reflection sessions can facilitate learning and performance by encouraging candid communication and self-assessment. This promotes a team-based culture of continuous improvement and learning, increasing productivity and quality.

Remain adaptable: Adaptable persons in their approach towards problem solving are better in overcoming difficulties and adapting to changing conditions. Adopt change and be ready to adjust your goals and tactics for whatever situations may require. Practice mindfulness exercises, like meditation or deep breathing, to stay in the present and respond coolly to unforeseen obstacles or changes of direction.

Begin with simple mindfulness practices such as body scans, mindful walking, or deep breathing in order to assist you in handling stress and anxiety. To enhance the management of stress and anxiety, practice mindfulness while performing your day-to-day activities.

Concentrate on finding solutions: Investigations have shown that problem-solving methods of coping have a link with good psychological adaptation and resilience. Answer seekers are able to report greater overall well-being and higher levels of satisfaction due to their searches.

Advice: Rather than focusing on problems, begin to consider possible solutions. Chunk down the problems and prioritize by impact and feasibility. Pursue the most attractive options with force, and adjust your tactics as needed.

All in all, the skills of reflection, adjustment, mindfulness, and problem-focused coping are the key to success in the contemporary workplace. Enforcing these strategies enables the people improve their productivity, adapt to changing situations, and maintain a positive attitude.

Recognition of progress, as well as celebration and reward, are known to yield higher levels of motivation, happiness, engagement and productivity in businesses. Have a gratitude jar or diary to list down what you have achieved and go through them periodically. Persistence and tenacity are key virtues to be successful in different areas such as academics, sports, and careers.

Development mindset is also important i.e. the people can learn and improve. Development-minded workers are more likely to seek feedback, accept responsibility for their mistakes, and be resilient at work. An example is a high school student who is poor in math but through questions, gained confidence in own abilities and knowledge of what is considered the potential and talent of such a person.

When these helpful suggestions and doable actions are implemented, a mindset that embraces challenges, learns from failures and achieves greater success and fulfilment can be developed. Resilience, self-kindness, and adaptability are the main components of overcoming challenges and winning. By practicing the notions in the daily routine one can accomplish the best in the personal and professional activities.

Chapter 4 : The Wealth of Well-Being

The author tells us about his own process of finding the link between well-being and financial prosperity. His journey was initiated by obsessive striving for success in the corporate world with the emphasis on material things and outside verification. Yet, he found out that the real wealth is not in what we have, but in how we live our lives and influence others.

To ensure well-being, he established the borders, employed self-kindness and fed his mind, body, and soul. He discovered that real wealth consists not only of material assets but also of physical health, emotional strength, and inner harmony. He embarked on a path of self- reflection and development, concentrating on nurturing the richness of wellness in all his life areas.

He redefined his success and started to take care of himself, choosing physical activity, mindful eating, and enough sleep as self-care practices, as well as personal development and lifelong learning, which involved mentorship and coaching.

While he was coming to comprehend wealth of well-being, he started to introduce the principles of abundance and generosity into his daily activities as apparently true satisfaction comes from sharing wealth with others and leaving a positive trace in world.

His path to financial prosperity and emotional and mental serenity started with the realization that real wealth is more than money. He changed his attention from superficial indicators like salary increases or materialistic rewards to overall development and personal satisfaction. Physical activity has also appeared in the spotlight as it influences the total physical health and exert a huge role both in mental and emotional well-being.

Mindfulness practice and meditation were also important elements of self-care that he used, to be in the moment and raise consciousness. Attending a weekend retreat that emphasized mindfulness and self-awareness refreshed his determination to focus on emotional and mental well-being.Nevertheless, although he continued to pay attention to self-care and personal development he saw the positive changes in most areas of his life, as he became more resilient, integrated and successful. He understood that success is not a destination, but an ongoing process of perfection and self-realization, rather than just an external recognition.

In two years of suffering and trials, the writer found out that tough conditions propels growth mindset . Accepting the lessons and finishing the job with a new energy, he found that true value is not in a bank account or a status, but in relationships, quality experiences and how an action aligns with values.

By emphasizing his well-being and the quality of his relationships, the wealth of his experiences and the congruence of his actions with values, his pleasure and contentment have increased significantly.

To guide and handle the abundance of well-being, readers should take care of themselves, develop emotional intelligence, manage stress successfully, create resilience, form nurturing relationships, establish boundaries, show gratitude and mindfulness, and seek support and professional help when required.

Schedule time for self-care activities like exercise, meditation, writing, and hobbies, establish a consistent sleep schedule, and practice mindful eating. Develop emotional intelligence by continuously monitoring your feelings, as well as the thoughts and beliefs that lay behind the surface. Effective stress management practices include mindfulness meditation, yoga, and tai chi, as well as creating a supportive workplace by setting limits and delegating duties.

Cultivate resilience by reframing failures as opportunities for growth and learning, concentrating on the things you can control, and appreciating the good fortune in your life. Cultivate meaningful connections by putting quality before quantity, mastering active listening and effective communication, and surrounding yourself with supportive people.

Readers will be able to make better decisions by using these practical advice, techniques, and action-oriented steps in their everyday lives.

Chapter 5: Building Meaningful Relationships.

In this chapter the author discussed that love, empathy, and vulnerability were critical for building real connections and active listening was necessary in this process because it was important in developing even stronger ones.

Vulnerability was also significant in the development of real connections since it is meant to provide a sanctuary for others to speak about their suffering and weaknesses. Nurturing those relationships over time demand continuous communication, nourishment, and celebration.

The quality of Relationship was found to be more relevant than quantity. The author emphasized sincere friendships, family unity and being able to forgive and forget. Self-care is also important because it enabled him to replenish the spirit and draw boundaries.

The author underlines the considerations of authentic, active listening, and vulnerability in development of the genuine connections. The acceptance of his limits, flaws and weaknesses allowed him to develop the stronger bonds and trust in the other people bringing joy and happiness.

To be truly present means to be authentic, and being authentic is a way of life, to be in a state of constant giving to your loving self. Genuine relationships are vital to our well-being and mental health. Being present and authentic takes effort, courage, and honesty.

True relationships are hard to create and maintain in the fast-paced world of to-day, but it is a virtue that must be protected. Accept your oddities, imperfections. Active listening is looking at the speaker, nodding, asking questions to show an interest in what they are saying. Vulnerability is not a weakness but a power.

Quality is better than quantity in the sense that we stay connected with our friends and families on a regular basis even though it may seem difficult to do so. Forgiveness is sometimes needed to get rid of negative energy and move on with an open heart. Boundaries are essential to keep relationships healthy because it allows us to be clear about our needs and communicate them assertively.Being real with people plays a significant role in our mental health and well-being. It gives a feeling of purpose and satisfaction because we have fun, laugh, and make memories with the people that we love. It brings happiness, satisfaction, and companionship that money and stuff will never be able to provide.

Briefly, the importance to develop and maintain true relationships in our life is focused on open communication, listening, empathy, and investing time and energy in long-term relationships which provide us with happiness and joy.

Chapter 6: Chapter 6: Financial Mindset Mastery

The wealth building psychology is a key factor for the long-term financial success. Wealth is a function of our financial psychology and releasing ourselves from constricting beliefs can allow us to reach our financial potential. Mark Cuban's case is an example of how a change in point of view can lead to wealth development. Cuban grew up in a middle-class family and has demonstrated early entrepreneurial qualities. He co-started Broadcast.com, which in turn was a great loss during the dot-com boom, in spite of his ordinary career path. He sold the business to Yahoo! in 1999, by more than $5.7 billion, and thus, the demonstration of his willingness to diversify his assets and take moderate risks.

During his wandering, Cuban found out how vital time, efficiency, and elasticity are in making wealth. One has to be ahead of the curve, embrace innovation, and never settle for less in order to succeed. Today, with a $4 billion net worth, Cuban ranks among the wealthiest people on the planet.

To create a healthy money mindset practice, abundance and gratitude, set clear financial goals, develop resilience, and use visualization and affirmations. A mentality of wealth, resilience, and calculated risk-taking can enable people to overcome obstacles and achieve their utmost financial objectives.

Affirmations and visualization help in attracting financial prosperity. Through harmonizing our subliminal mind with our conscious aspirations, we can create a solid base for our financial goals. Notable characters who have used visualization and affirmation include Jim Carrey, who is an actor and a comedian, and Oprah Winfrey, a media mogul and philanthropist.

Employing constant visualization and affirmations, Winfrey developed a multimedia empire and fulfilled her financial goals, which made her as a television show star. Positive affirmations and picturing himself being a great actor also helped Carrey in his acting accomplishments.

In the modern rapidly changing economy, lifelong learning is vital to remain competitive and updated. By seeking possibilities for financial education and skill development, these could be in the form of books, classes, or mentorship.

Benjamin Graham, a well-known investor and the author of "The Intelligent Investor", had an influence on the great investor Frank Buffett. Buffett was the only one to have achieved an unmatched financial success thanks to his systematic investment approach and commitment to lifelong learning, which brought Berkshire Hathaway to life, one of the biggest as well as most profitable companies in the world.

In short, affirmations and visualization are powerful techniques for achieving monetary prosperity. People can prosper in their financial lives by looking for opportunities for skill development and having the growth mindset in relation to financial education.

Sara Blakely, the founder of Spanx, is a wealthy woman businesswoman who grew up in Clearwater, Florida, and had to work several jobs to pay for her education. Blakely appreciated creativity and innovative approach to solving problems and at the same time, she was aware that education would help her achieve her entrepreneurial dreams. Blakely's perseverance to gain success and her undying love for learning never died out even when challenges and rejections presented themselves.

It was clear that Blakely's dedication to education and her entrepreneurial spirit had paid-off when she introduced her revolutionary shapewear brand, Spanx, in 2000. Blakely's innovative invention as well as her clever marketing tactics made Spanx a huge success, despite the opposition from the investors and the retailers. This also made her the youngest self-made female billionaire in history.

Those who fear failure and loss must admit and manage this fear to overcome it and take calculated risks as they seek financial success. Other strategies for risk management are a fair attitude towards risk, careful planning and diversification, and focusing like a laser on long-term objectives.

Elon Musk, the visionary multimillionaire who created SpaceX, Tesla, and Neuralink, is famous for his daring financial endeavors. Musk's venture into space exploration and Tesla's re-establishment of the auto industry endorsed his goal to present space exploration to the general public and consolidate his position as a space industry leader.

The company values of SpaceX and Tesla today are in billions of dollars, and the boldness of Musk to challenge uncertainty, gamble on odds, and overturn established customs did change the course of several industries as well as inspired many others to pursue their own dreams of innovation and wanderlust.

Elon Musk and best-selling Harry Potter author J.K. Rowling are two examples of persons who defeated fear and took bold financial risks to pursue their pastimes. Rowling had to refuse many offers from publishers before she eventually signed a contract for "Harry Potter and the Philosopher's Stone", the first of her books. Rowling gave her all to develop the Harry Potter books, even though she was only paid a £1,500 advance for the first book in the series. In addition, she also suffered a huge financial gamble for doing so.

J.K. Rowling and Elon Musk reached immense success and their legacy is still motivating people to dare to take risks and follow their dreams, by overcoming their fears, accepting uncertainty and with a lot of passion and dedication in what they love.

We are under the influence of social networks regarding our financial behaviors and approaches. Living with or associating ourselves with likeminded people who are of similar beliefs and aspirations, we create an atmosphere that is conductive to success and financial fortune. Building relationships with people who have the same values with you can facilitate advancement and success for both .

The Bangladeshi economist and social entrepreneur Muhammad Yunus is well recognized for his revolutionary work in micro financing and poverty reduction. Yunus gave poor women especially the opportunity to break out of poverty by giving them small loans and community support through his revolutionary Grameen Bank concept.

The community-based financial education through Dave Ramsey, a radio host and personal finance guru, has empowered millions of people to take control of their finances and attain their fiscal goals.

Thankfulness and giving to others are two of wealth creating ingredients as they initiate an abundant cycle that yields good fortune for us and others around us. Incorporating kindness, gratitude, or giving into our financial rituals allows us to be in rhythm with the flow of abundance and attract more wealth in our life. Thankfulness and charity are parts of this. Notable people among them Oprah Winfrey and Bill Gates have shown the wonderful power of giving and gratitude upon the people and communities.

Attaining long-term wealth and abundance involves learning the money mindset. By knowing the psychology of financial creation and developing an empowered attitude and habit, we will be able to see our highest potential and create the life we want. By implementing the ideas presented here, we stand to actualize our greatest potential and create the life of our dreams.

To reach financial and material prosperity and security, one needs to be patient and goal-oriented. When we start a business, buy a house, or plan for retirement, our success is significantly enhanced by a clear plan and executable strategies.

Financial goal setting and meeting is important success factors in the fashion industry. Inventor of Spanx, Sara Blakely, revolutionized the underwear industry through the creation of form-fitting, comfortable shapewear products for women. She measured such key performance indicators as sales revenue, market share, and customer satisfaction to keep track of her progress. Blakely developed a comprehensive plan, which included consumer participation, marketing, distribution, and product development. She gave research and development investment to manufacture top quality textiles and designs that were appealing to customers.

Tactics that were applicable to this market, like celebrity endorsements, a targeted marketing strategy, and clever alliances with retailers, helped Spanx to dominate the market. Blakely set tight timelines for new products, market growth, and revenue targets.In order to achieve, your financial goals must be clear, sequenced in terms of importance and time, broken down into smaller objectives, budgeted realistically, and automated through savings and investments. Harvard Business Review research shows that individuals who write down their goals are 42% more likely to achieve their goals than those who do not. Positive goal framing can increase motivation and determination, promoting activity and progress of the goal. You can reset your financial trajectory and achieve your long-term objectives by introducing these strategies.

Chapter 7 : Cultivating Progress and Personal Growth

The author talked about a way of constant improvement and personal growth, and the importance of self-assessment and self-improvement. He started by a hardcore self-assessment, looking back at his previous experiences, as well as peer and mentors feedback. He then carried out self-assessment activities with the help of tools such as personality tests, skill inventories, and SWOT analyses to review his strengths and areas in which he should work on.

The author established specific, measurable, achievable, relevant, and time-bound (SMART) goals as per his overall goals aimed at areas for improvement. He created a customized growth plan highlighting practical actions required to meet these objectives, with specific approaches to maximize their strengths, overcome weaknesses, and seize growth opportunities.

Additionally, the author devised a structured schema based on the steps and the measures that should be accomplished to reach them. He disassembled each goal into smaller tasks, in order to make progress, he set deadlines and accountability measures. He located resources and support networks like training programs, work shops, courses or mentoring facilities, which would help him to attain his goals creatively.

To see his development, he made a visual plan or timeline which could be Gantt chart, project management tool or simple checklist. Continuous review and assessment enabled him to remain agile and adaptive to the changing conditions, without losing sight of his objectives.

His methodical process of self-evaluation, self-analyzation, and a planned approach for continuous improvement has contributed significantly towards his success and the attainment of his objectives. This approach offers clarity, accountability, and motivation to him that allows him to have a consistent progress on his goals and constant improvement in all aspects of his life.

The author's concept of continuous improvement was associated with lifelong learning, professional advancement, and personal development. He looked for ways of advancement in his professional growth by means of education including workshops and self-study, staying informed of the industry trends and the best practices. He was focused on the development of the personality and on the well-being and adapted some healthy habits, such as sports and practice of mindfulness. He was flexible and responsive to critics, and saw challenges as a way of learning.

Gradually, he noticed the concrete results in productivity, efficiency, and overall comfort and satisfaction with his work and life. He was dedicated and focused and stayed true to his path, making considerable headway towards his targets.

To have a clear record of the progress, he set specific performance indicators for each goal and milestone. He employed different tracking tools and systems which included some project management software, spreadsheets, or pen-and-paper approaches to control the course of events. Checkpoint at regular intervals were established to discuss progress and issues of deviation from the plan.

Achievement celebration was a structural component of the tracking system, which permitted him to evaluate his success and build motivation. He thanked and acknowledged those who backed him, thus enhancing his support system. He would once in a while treat himself after completion of important milestones or goals.

A growth mindset kept him attentive to his long-term goals and in dealing with the challenges. He managed to keep the momentum to reach his goals .

Holistic prosperity is more than money and represents a well-being of a person in terms of physical health, mental stability, satisfactory relations with other people, continuous self-development and meaningful involvement in society. Names such as Oprah Winfrey, Elon Musk, Michelle Obama, Richard Branson, Malala Yousafzai, Dalai Lama, Serena Williams, Nelson Mandela, Ellen DeGeneres, and Mahatma Gandhi have been highlighted as an exhibit of this path.

Oprah Winfrey's stresses on the development of wholeness from inside, advocating wellness products, books, and spiritual teachings. Elon Musk manages his high ambition with self care and integrates exercise, proper nutrition, and practices of mindfulness into his routine. Michelle Obama promotes real contacts by highlighting empathy, compassion, and mutual help. Richard Branson appreciates lifelong learning and constant challenges and does not limit himself to only one interest. Malala Yousafzai is a source of inspiration by her activities in favor of girls' education and human rights.

The Dalai Lama personifies inner peace, compassion, and mindfulness, uplifting millions all over the world. The fact that Serena Williams has excelled on the court and has countless accolades does not make her only focus on professional growth, but she also looks at her growth in other aspects of her life. Nelson Mandela embodies the principles of forgiveness, determination, and harmony in the realization of comprehensive prosperity. Ellen DeGeneres' talk show is a host to happiness and good will. He champions for social causes and gives aid to humanitarian organizations. The name of Mahatma Gandhi represents the ideas of simplicity, truthfulness, and non-violence as ways to the general wellbeing.

These characters provide us with powerful lessons about what a balanced joyful life in our fast moving world should be.

Holistic prosperity includes such needs as self-care priority, ambition and self-care balance, meaningful relationship investment, lifelong learning, contribution to society, inner peace cultivation, success and self-care accommodation, forgiveness and resilience practice, joy and kindness spread, simplicity and truth embrace. The likes of Holistic prosperous people include persons such as Oprah Winfrey, Elon Musk, Michelle Obama, Richard Branson, Malala Yousafzai, the

Dalai Lama, Serena Williams, Nelson Mandela, Ellen DeGeneres, and Mahatma Gandhi. Incorporating these practical principles into our lives, we can create a life of harmony and meaning, and this leads to contentment.

BEFORE YOU GO

YOUR VOICE MATTERS

P LEASE, SPARE A MINUTE to rate this book using the star ratings from 1-to-5, that usually pops up at the end of this publication. I appreciate your honest feedback, positive or negative. And if you have an extra moment to spare, could you rate the book on Amazon.

Thank you, and best regards.

Manjul

Special Note:

As most e book readers (including the Amazon Kindle) do not have a great internet browser interface, you might prefer to scan the QR Code below using your smart phone.

Scan the QR Code with your smart phone and put a rating or a review

Preview of book "The Clear Mindset "

C HAPTER 1 Unveiling the Overthinking Paradox

Overthinking paradox is a complicated issue that concerns people as well as professionals. It dates back to early humans, who used it as a prediction and way to plan for future dangers. However, in the contemporary world, this quality has become a cumbersome problem and a self-created complication.

This paradox is evident in different aspects, including decision-making deadlock, relationship tensions, blocked creativity, problems with emotional wellbeing, and physical symptoms such as lack of sleep, headaches, and muscle pain. In addition, overthinking can act as a trigger for emotional turmoil, anxiety, and physiological issues that affect the health of humans.

In order to overcome the overthinking paradox, it is essential for an individual to introduce self-awareness instead of getting bogged down in constant thinking and evaluating. In order to get out of this involved and elaborate game of over-thinking, people should first identify where it happens the most often and what causes it.

Adopting mindfulness would enable you to remain focused and provide additional space from the complicated pattern of overthinking. With achievable goals, tasks can be de-simplified and lean on the mind. Decision-making without overanalysing and setting a time frame helps to avoid the paralysis of too much thinking. Setting boundaries creates more mental space for people and helps them deal with an overload-rich world.

Gratitude practice negates the negative and creates the positive. The maze of the overthinking paradox can be navigated by seeking support from friends, family, or professionals. Physical activity can alleviate physical symptoms and contribute to good mental health.

By adopting a growth mindset, people can look at challenges as opportunities for gaining knowledge and personal development, where failures are transformed into advantages.

In conclusion, freeing ourselves from the overthinking paradox is a potential accomplishment that can be realized through self-reflection and perseverance. If the paradox becomes clear and a person realizes it, then its power is gone. The intricate web of overthinker could be conquered by willpower and techniques.

Chapter 2 Rewiring Your Mental Landscape

The process of rewiring an individual's mental landscape is an evolving journey and not just a spontaneous act. Cognitive restructuring, affirmations, visualization, gratitude, and mindfulness are techniques that will help form a new mental foundation that has been transformed into one full of a positive mindset. Cognitive behavioural therapy (CBT) is, therefore, aiming to make permanent changes to the way one thinks.

The use of positive affirmations acts as beacons to construct new philosophy, improving belief alignment through positive remarks that have been proven effective during research. Visualization involves mental rehearsal for plotting out success and coming up with solutions to problems The daily gratitude practice acts towards reorienting stress. At least three weeks of mindfulness training, involving meditation and other breathing control exercises, yields specific neuro-structural changes with better attention, emotional control, and a reduction in negative thoughts.

A growth mindset includes redefinition and attribution, where the problem is not a weakness but a chance for learning. In terms of self-verbalization and levels of internal communication, self-esteem improves when one is engaged in the use of positive self-talk, which could be, "You've got this" and "every challenge is an opportunity. The new thought patterns are heavily influenced by surrounding oneself with positivity, connecting to positive people, inspiration, positive motivation, and goals. Clarity journaling involves recording the patterns that are involved in the true moments of mindfulness.

Successful mental rewiring depends on constant learning and adaptation. Integration of technology in mental health interventions is another field that has a lot of potential. Even by means of mobile apps and virtual platforms, one can have guided mindfulness sessions, cognitive restructuring exercises, and positive psychology interventions to create mind rewiring.

Chapter 3 : Conquering the Doubt Demon

Self-doubt is an important area of life that goes through a number of stages. One way is to develop self-awareness to identify patterns of negative self-talk which erode self-esteem. To build confidence, the goals should be realistic, rewards, upon attainment of success however small it may be, be given. Accepting that no matter how much we put in our work, it will never be perfect can help release the burden of trying to make everything flawless. In relation to self-doubt, there is always the chance for constant improvement and resilience to be shown.

Consulting people close to us may challenge any negative thoughts and allow one to concentrate on the present moment. Being in the moment and avoiding trappings in the mind can be achieved through mindfulness, as well as breathing practices.

Perfection is a bourgeoisie concept; hence, perfect quality can only exist for the bourgeoisies themselves and it exists at any time if one desires to have it, but it also dies when one decides that he has no need in it. Eliminating thoughts of negativity and self-doubt requires avoiding comparing oneself with other people too much as well as using inappropriate self-talk. To facilitate the process, individuals need professional guidance during the implementation of cognitive-behavioral approaches, mindfulness-based interventions, positive psychology interventions, personal strength building, and understanding the importance of compassion.

Studies indicate that application of cognitive-behavioral approaches, mindfulness-based interventions, positive psychology interventions, personal strength building, and numerous therapeutic techniques can aid in moving beyond self-doubt. In addition to that, receiving professional help, visualizing targets, acknowledging breakthroughs and embracing inadequacies will also serves as a weapon to fight self-doubt.

Chapter 4 : Stress Detox: A Holistic Approach

In our present-day life, we live at such a tremendous speed that stress and strain invade it and affect our peace of mind, resulting in sleepless nights and restless days. An alternative to these approaches is the holistic style, which suggests that stressors are the result of cognitive imbalances and therefore they can be solved by determining cognitive imbalances. This includes building a lifestyle that promotes resilience.

Such holistic lifestyle changes include mindful mornings, therapy of exercise, nutrition for nourishment, digital detox, boundaries for balance, reflection, quality sleep rituals, task prioritization, mindful breaks, practice gratitude, area of communication and support, and learning delegation.

When stress is holistically approached, it is transformed into constructive change and growth. Hence, it is critical to properly manage anxious thoughts through practical tips accompanied by their dealing and action steps.

For a comprehensive scientific approach, integration technology into mental health interventions could also be beneficial for stress detox. The comprehensive way to relieve from stress is to develop resilience, prevent another return, and plan for long-term well-being rather than to seek for short-term relief.

All in all, stress may not be treated alone but the cause and the known stressor must be attended so as to remove them. Holistic approach enables individuals to deal with the complexities of stress and eliminate its effects through lifestyle modification.

Chapter 5: Mindful Living Art

Mindfulness is the way to inner peace and balance. Morning rituals are usually considered to be some boring acts that we engage in to start off our day e.g. having our cup of tea, but they can turn out to be sacred rituals where we feel thanks for every sensation. As a form of mindfulness, walking meditation can also be related to this condition where one has to concentrate on one step at a time and the external surroundings.

Here, people may develop 'breath as the life line' to promote inner silence in the face of these disturbances of the mind, listen to one's thoughts 'without judgment' and practice mindful eating. The traditional philosophy of fast food is replaced by an enjoyment of the taste and the texture of the meal which engages all the senses and thus introduces the slow food attitude.

Mindfulness is a ripple effect – from the self to society changing acts of kindness to expressions of connection. the mindful choice of people to protect our planet helps them to keep their personal welfare and to preserve the environment. Every single decision made about environmental conservation is a responsible choice.

Living mindfully is a continuous awakening, where beauty is in each second of life, and it is peace inside and thankfulness for every moment. Every day is a day of significance, relatedness and tranquillity; Achieved by the strength of now.

Some practical behaviours that promote a balanced life include mindful breathing, mindful morning rituals, mindful walking, mindful eating behaviour, tech-free zones, mindful listening, mindfulness in daily tasks, mindful pauses, gratitude practice, mindful movement, mindful evening rituals, mindfulness workshops, and similar societal groups.

A mindful life is a life in balance and never ends or saturates. It is woven into the tissue of the life, and it carries harmony, vision, and profound wellness.

Chapter 6: Emotional Alchemy: The Change of Negativity into Positivity

The Crucible of Despair becomes the one of the agents of change and allows a person to see challenges as growth and emotional alchemy. These practices comprise of mindful awareness of feelings, cognitive reappraisal of experiences, appreciation amidst difficult times, self-kindness and shared humanity, and doing good facilitated by support and connection. The emotional alchemy is a perpetual process, transforming us from suffering to resilience.

Some of the practice-based emotional transformation steps include mindful awareness, re-scripting for resilience and empowerment, developing gratitude in the face of adversity, embracing self-compassion, active participation in positive actions, support and connection via various processes, mind-body practices for emotional well being, reflection and optimism through journaling and visualization, creation of emotional boundaries, culture of continuous learning.

Chapter 7 : Releasing: The Strength that Flows from Letting Go

To release is an intentional action to free oneself from emotional loads, stimulate self-care and liberate from past weights. It includes the practice of forgiving, letting go of impermanence, giving up the control, journaling the release, mindfulness meditation, being grateful, creating emotional boundaries, and self-care.

Forgiveness is the starting point for letting go, and writing a forgiveness letter helps by giving acknowledgment and conscious release. Surrender to impermanence release from attachment to both outcomes and relationships, and mindfulness meditation aids concentration on the temporary nature of everything. Letting go of the control is the way to liberation where the control is consciously released. Writing down the release and picturing events assist the mind in emotional release.

Whereas mindfulness meditation trains awareness and presence, gratitude modifies the perception from negative to positive. Setting emotional limits ensures emotional health and eliminates both drama and hanging on. Visualization techniques promote lightness and freedom, whereas seeking professional help is necessary for coping with profound emotional issues.

Letting go is the necessity of self-care, and its attention in the schedule allows a freer state of mind. Letting go journey is a continuous one with each step a win of strength and self-love. The key is to shape a lighter, more flexible head so as not to be locked up in the past.

Chapter 8 : Emotional Armoring

Strength and resilience are not instant as development of these includes qualities such as self discipline, persistence, awareness, vulnerability, and determination to keep progress. The other critical constituents include self-compassion, gratitude and empathy the ability to comprehend the emotions of others.

BOOKS BY THE SAME AUTHOR

BOOKS BY THE SAME AUTHOR

5   The Innovative Mindset

https://www.amazon.com/Innovativ
e-Mindset-Innovation-Creativity-
Innovators-ebook/dp/B0CI98N8M2

6   The Eloquent Mindset

https://www.amazon.com/dp/
B0CM5D3VW1

7   The Clear Mindset

https://www.amazon.com/dp
/B0CSSQ3MC6/

ABOUT THE AUTHOR

Manjul Tewari, a blogger, best-selling author, and versatile writer, is the creative force behind the captivating 'Mindset Mastery Series' available on Amazon.

With an engaging and informative style, Manjul's writings transcend conventional boundaries, enriching the lives of readers worldwide. Delve deeper into Manjul's literary world and discover the transformational power of effective communication and mindset mastery.

Visit the **author's profile on Amazon** to explore the full range of captivating works. Uncover the magic of communication and mindset mastery through the lens of Manjul Tewari's literary adventure.

REFERENCES

- "The Power of Positive Thinking" by Norman Vincent Peale

- "Mindset: The New Psychology of Success" by Carol S. Dweck

- "The Happiness Advantage: How a Positive Brain Fuels Success in Work and Life" by Shawn Achor

- "The How of Happiness: A New Approach to Getting the Life You Want" by Sonja Lyubomirsky

- "Positive Intelligence: Why Only 20% of Teams and Individuals Achieve Their True Potential and How You Can Achieve Yours" by Shirzad Chamine

- "Positivity: Top-Notch Research Reveals the Upward Spiral That Will Change Your Life" by Barbara Fredrickson